The Sound of Listening

A Retreat Journal from Thomas Merton's Hermitage

JOHN DEAR, S.J.

Continuum • New York

1999

The Continuum Publishing Company
370 Lexington Avenue
New York, NY 10017

Photo of Thomas Merton's hermitage by
Alan Gilmore, Abbey of Gethsemani

Printed in the United States of America

Library of Congress Cataloging-in-Publication Data

Dear, John
    The sound of listening : a retreat journal from Thomas Merton's
hermitage / John Dear
        p.   cm.
    ISBN 0-8264-1189-4 (pbk.)
    1. Merton, Thomas, 1915–1968 Meditations. 2. Retreats. 3. Dear,
John, 1959–   Diaries. I. Title
    BX4705.M542D43   1999
    269'.6—dc21   99-291050
                                                             CIP

The Sound of Listening

For Brother Patrick Hart

Our real journey in life is interior; it is a matter of growth, deepening, and of an ever greater surrender to the creative action of love and grace in our hearts. Never was it more necessary for us to respond to that action.

—*Thomas Merton*

Contents

Introduction

Few Catholic Christians except perhaps John XXIII, John Paul II, Dorothy Day, and Mother Teresa have made as great an impact upon the twentieth century as Thomas Merton, the celebrated Trappist monk, poet, author, and critic who died in Bangkok on December 10, 1968, twenty-seven years to the day after he entered the Abbey of Gethsemani near Louisville, Kentucky.

After publishing one of the most widely read religious autobiographies of all times, *The Seven Storey Mountain*, and writing countless poems and over fifty books of spiritual reflection and political critique, Merton retreated further in the early 1960s to a small hermitage built just over a mile from the monastery on a hill in the middle of the woods. There he spent what were to be his last years, fervently writing urgent essays on nuclear disarmament, nonviolence, racial equality, social justice, civil rights,

Gandhi, Vietnam, and Buddhism. There he received some of the leading figures of the times, people like Thich Nhat Hanh, Daniel Berrigan, Joan Baez, Jacques Maritain, Denise Levertov, John Howard Griffin, and Czeslaw Milosz. In March, 1968, he prepared to welcome Martin Luther King, Jr. for retreat—until he received news of Dr. King's assassination. Merton had stepped further apart from the world, becoming the first "public" hermit in modern Christian history, and yet, in doing so, he reached out farther into the world than ever before.

At the heart of Merton's voluminous message emerges a simple invitation to peel away our illusions and violence and come together in peace and truth before the living God. For Merton, the spiritual life was life itself—pure and simple. Because he spent his days grounded in prayer (with at least seven hours for private meditation and community prayer each day for twenty-seven years), Merton experienced God's presence everywhere. He became a true mystic, and because he sought God so authentically, listened so faithfully, and loved so deeply, he was compelled to proclaim the truth of peace and justice to the world. He became a prophet to the nation, and as such, was duly dismissed.

Merton knew that the God of life wants us to live life to the fullest and to let others live life abundantly as well. His prayer pushed him out to the world with an urgent appeal to stop the wars, abolish nuclear weapons, overcome racism, eradicate poverty, and wake up to the reality and unity of human existence. His message was deeply spiritual because it was profoundly political. That is to say, it broke loose of any categories or ideologies: it was human to the core.

Perhaps the greatest joy in Merton's last years was the freedom he discovered in the hermitage that the community built for him in 1960. A simple three room cinder block structure, it sits on the edge of a sloping field, nestled among pine trees and woods. The main room features a large window looking out at the field and a great stone fireplace. In these simple rooms, Merton prayed, wrote, laughed, and lived.

Merton's hermitage still stands today, a quiet place for retreat and meditation on holy ground. Since his untimely death in 1968, the hermitage has been used by monks of the community for week-long private retreats. It is not usually open to the public and remains hidden away in the hills.

In mid-November, 1996, I spent nine days on retreat at the Abbey of Gethsemani. Through the hospitality and generosity of the Trappist community, particularly Brother Patrick Hart and the abbot, Father Timothy Kelly, I was able to stay in Merton's secluded hermitage.

The pages that follow give an account of those quiet days of solitude, silence, and intimacy with the God of peace. I arrived that November afternoon exhausted from a relentless year and half as the Executive Director of the Sacred Heart Center, a community center for low-income families in the impoverished Southside section of Richmond, Virginia. Serving nearly five hundred people a day, the Sacred Heart Center offers a variety of programs, including a licensed day care program for two and a half to five year olds; after school and summer programs; a Family Resource Program (with academic training and parenting skills for adult women and child care for their children); an adolescents' program; employment opportunities for local residents; emergency fuel and food assistance; kindergarten, first and second grade classes each for twelve at-risk children; a parents' support group; a lay health-workers program; classes for new or expecting mothers; and various recreational opportunities and community events. By working directly with neighborhood children and parents to meet their specific needs, the center strikes at the roots of violence and poverty.

Though my work focused on fundraising, administration, personnel management, and public relations, I spent most of my time trying to fix the leaky roof, the broken bus, or the ever-flooding bathroom. By the time my religious superiors decided to send me to my Jesuit tertianship year (a year of study and renewal, culminating in final vows), I felt quite burnt-out. At the same time, two close relationships had ruptured. Tired and despairing, I pulled up to the monastery seeking relief. I received much more.

"The contemplative life must provide an area, a space of liberty, of silence, in which possibilities are allowed to surface and new choices—beyond routine choice—become manifest," Merton writes. "It should create a new experience of time . . . one's own time, but not dominated by one's own ego and its demands; hence, open to others, compassionate time."

Merton calls us to discover "the happiness of being at one with everything in the hidden ground of Love for which there can be no explanations," and that "what is important in nonviolence is the contemplative truth that is not seen. The radical truth of reality is that we are all one." Merton plumbed the spiritual depths of the truth of human unity by entering the solitude of his own heart, safe in the woods of Gethsemani in his concrete hermitage.

After a few hours in those quiet rooms, I too began to feel a new inner peace and freedom. It seemed as if the peace of God's own presence had descended upon me in the silence. Those days remain with me, deep in my heart. I hope to remain faithful to the gift of those days, to go forward into the world with a listening heart and a word of peace and love, truth and nonviolence, rooted, like Merton, in the silence of God, in the peace of Christ.

"The contemplative life has nothing to tell you except to reassure you and say that if you dare to penetrate your own silence and dare to advance without fear into the solitude of your own heart," Merton tells us, "you will truly recover the light and capacity to understand what is beyond words and beyond explanations because it is too close to be explained."

I hope these pages, this little journal, will encourage us all to pursue that inner recovery, the holy journey into the peace of God.

JOHN DEAR, S.J.

Saturday, November 16, 1996

The clear blue sky shines brightly across West Virginia and Kentucky as I make my way to the hidden hills near Bardstown. I get lost driving along the country roads when suddenly the large, white monastery appears on my left. I see the lower, dark grey wall, a remnant of the original cloister, and the dark pointed church bell tower with the cross on top. I pull up to the front entrance and take a deep breath.

Today marks the seventh anniversary of the assassination of six Jesuits and their coworkers, Elba and Celina Ramos, at the Jesuit University in San Salvador, El Salvador. I remember visiting with them throughout the summer of 1985, when I had gone to work in a church-sponsored refugee camp in El Salvador. I remember the pictures of their bloody, lifeless bodies lying face down on the front lawn of the community house. With Jesuits and friends in the San Francisco Bay Area, where I was studying at the Jesuit School of Theology in Berkeley, I spoke out for an end to United States military aid to El Salvador. A month after those murders, just before Christmas, 1989, I made my first pilgrimage here to Gethsemani. I came tired and devastated, and shortly I found new strength in the peace of the monastic life.

Once again, on this important anniversary, I come to the Abbey of Gethsemani. I arrive tired and spiritually drained. I come to recenter my soul in Christ. I think of the many Jesuits and friends from around the country who gather today for prayer and nonviolent civil disobedience at the gates of the School of the Americas in Georgia, calling for the closure of that military training center for death squad troops in Latin America. The soldiers who killed the Jesuits and their coworkers, as well as the four North American churchwomen and even Archbishop Romero, were trained in Georgia. I pray with my friends for the immediate closing of this "School of Assassins."

Yesterday, I visited my father at Georgetown University hospital. His leg is reddish and swollen, but steadily healing from a sudden and serious infection, which is related to the removal of a vein for his heart by-pass surgery last January. His spirits are good, though his energy has been depleted. He expects to go home tomorrow and encouraged me to go on ahead to Kentucky. A real survivor, he has overcome colon and liver cancer, angioplasties, heart by-pass surgery, and now a serious leg infection. He remains in my heart and prayers every moment.

I walk along the monastery wall to the cemetery below the church bell tower where Thomas Merton rests with his brother monks under the shade of a huge cedar tree. At his grave, before a short white cross, I offer a prayer that these days may be filled with peace and prayer, that I may turn to Christ with all my heart, that I may become an instrument of Christ's peace. I look up at the clear blue sky. The breeze refreshes me. I walk back slowly and enter the monastery.

I want to start with a clean slate. In the guest house, a sign invites retreatants to receive the Sacrament of Reconciliation. I wait in line in the chapel. I confess my sins. A compassionate monk listens attentively. He calls me back to the basics, to the love of Christ and the roots of my vocation.

St. Francis's peace prayer offers a framework for my confession. I begin: I have not been an instrument of the Lord's peace. Parts of me have been sowing hatred, instead of love; despair instead of hope; darkness instead of light; doubt instead of faith; sorrow instead of joy. I seek my own consolation instead of consoling others; arrogantly insist that I be understood instead of understanding others; and demand to be loved instead of generously loving others. It's the same old story. My heart has grown cold. I feel burnt-out, far from God. I take responsibility for myself. I've become exceedingly proud, selfish, ungrateful, narcicisstic, thoughtless, hurtful, even violent. I have not loved as I could, have not believed as I should, and have not hoped as I would. God have mercy on me on a sinner.

As my penance the priest suggests a quiet, prayerful reading of Psalm 139:

> Yahweh, you have probed me and you know me; you know when I sit and when I stand; you understand my thoughts from afar. My journeys and my rest you scrutinize, with all my ways you are familiar. . . . Behind me and before, you hem me in and rest your hand upon me. Such knowledge is too wonderful for me; too lofty for me to attain. . . . Your eyes have seen my actions; in your book they are all written; my days were limited before one of them existed. How weighty are your designs, O God; how vast the sum of them!

I have arrived.

Sunday

Whh at a shock to wake up as the monks do at 3 A.M. I stumble into the church at 4:15 A.M. for the hour long "Vigils" service. As the psalms are sung, the words seep in. Their call to God for help resonates within me. Their sorrow, their gratitude, their joy become my own. A monk reads the Gospel. The disciples walk along the road to Emmaus and, without realizing it, meet the risen Christ. He explains the scriptures, the coming of the Messiah, the necessity of suffering love in the grand scheme of salvation. Their hearts burn as he speaks. Finally, they recognize him in the breaking of the bread.

A monk concludes with a prayer asking for the joy of the risen Lord and a share in his resurrection. This is what I need and what I seek this week: a sharing in the Lord's joy, in the Lord's resurrection, new life, and the peace of the risen Jesus.

Come, Lord, take me to you. Bring me into the new life of your resurrection. Lift me out of my selfishness, my despair, my faithlessness, my fear. Let me know the joy of your resurrection. Help me to see you along the way, in the scriptures, in the breaking of the bread. Let my heart burn with your abiding presence.

I am slowly transformed. My old self, my old shell, cracks and falls off. My spirit begins to breathe again. I am being reborn.

5:30 A.M. I am a man dying of thirst, crawling through the desert. Suddenly, a cool drink! Consolation! I contemplate the road to Emmaus Gospel story. Imagine the Lord explaining what happened to him! My heart burns in his presence and recognizes him in the breaking of the bread. The Lord appears in my meditation and quietly whispers over and over again, "I have brought you here . . . to share my joy . . . to give you my peace . . . to know my love . . . to strengthen you." I ponder the image of Christ—smiling, joyful, welcoming, inviting, looking at me with love. I feel rejuvenated!

The monks were not expecting me until today, but last night, they generously gave me a room in the third floor of the South wing of the main building, which used to be the old infirmary, one of the few places during the 1940s and 1950s where Merton found solitude before he moved to his hermitage.

Last night, one of the monks showed a video to the cluster of retreatants about the Trappist Order and the Abbey of Gethsemani. He spoke glowingly of the Abbot, Fr. Timothy Kelly, who has held the office for twenty-four years. Fr. Timothy shares all the duties and work of ordinary monks (including the laborious cheese and fruitcake manufacturing). He also supervises Gethsemani's six "daughter" houses around the world. He has made over a hundred visits to these other monasteries and, at the moment, is visiting the Abbey of the Holy Cross in Berryville, Virginia. During each visitation, he meets one-on-one with each monk. If he has concerns for the monastery, he writes to the Abbot General in Rome.

I see a little more clearly now the anguish that has been the last three years—my eight months in jail for my Plowshares anti-nuclear action (1993–94); the long months of house arrest in Washington, D.C. (1994–95); and the stress of the Sacred Heart Center in Richmond (1995 to the present). A great unhappiness, depression, and tension have pervaded these months. But now I am turning a corner. Surely life at the West Side Jesuit Community in New York City and my time here at Gethsemani will be crucial to this turning, this rejuvenation of my soul. I love the Sacred Heart Center and the people of the neighborhood, but it is time to leave Richmond, and the leave-taking is painful.

These past few weeks, I have wandered the streets of New York City and shared quiet evenings with Jesuit friends at the West Side Community. New York City is brimming with life, activity, noise, and people of all kinds. I take a daily walk in the park, keep a regimen of prayer, meditation, and bible study, and spend quality time with the gentle and kindly Jesuits of the community. It is a blessing to be in such good company.

After Terce, I had a good long visit with my friend Brother Patrick Hart, who first invited me to the monastery in 1989. So full of life, so warm, gracious, kind, interested, telling me about the monastery and the church. He spoke of the Dalai Lama's visit here a few months back for an international conference on Christian-Buddhist dialogue. "Merton was the first to show me the contemplative side of Christianity," the Dalai Lama told the monks. At the end, the Dalai Lama and the Abbot planted a pine tree along the wall at the front entrance of the monastery. Patrick also spoke of his work in recent years editing the seven volumes of Thomas Merton's journals and the ongoing interest in Merton's writings. Also, he told me how the community has welcomed a young Mexican Trappistine nun who has lived in community with the monks for over a year now. The community, including the Abbot General in Rome, has shown great hospitality to her.

At seventy-one, Patrick is filled with energy and spunk. After forty-five years at Gethsemani, he exudes happiness, joy, and a love of life. I am grateful to be with him again.

I call my father. He is all right, after a restless night, and hopes to go home from the hospital today.

I return to my monastic cell and finish reading Wes Howard-Brook's important new commentary, *John's Gospel and the Renewal of the Church*. John's Gospel must be understood within its social-political context, Wes insists, as well as our own, if we are to unpack its message. Wes explains how John's Gospel challenges the Christian community to choose love over power, the spirit over the letter of the law. John calls us to walk the way of the cross to death and resurrection, to practice the life of radical discipleship, Wes rightly concludes. "As we continue our discipleship journey in a troubled and confused world," he writes, "we can only hope that the Johannine memory of Jesus can persist in challenging the church to remember that obedience is rooted in listening, that prayerful openness to the Spirit who continues to blow freely, wherever God wills." Instead of "an over-spiritualized" pious text, John's Gospel is an urgent summons to radical, selfless love, even unto death, for the sake of humanity. I put the book down and ponder the invitation of discipleship to Jesus. Can I live a life of radical, self-giving love?

During Mass, Fr. Matthew Kelty preaches a scathing attack on the United States. After reading Jesus' parable about the master who entrusts his property to three servants and how the first two are rewarded for their work, but not the third (Mt 25:14–30), he tells us first about *Fortune* magazine's recent list of the hundred wealthiest people in the country, each of whom possesses at least $450 million. One is a candle maker who "made it" by cornering the church market. There are nearly two million millionaires in the United States, the monk observes. Meanwhile, one out of five children in the United States suffers in misery below the poverty level. The top 20 percent of the global population controls 80 percent of the world's resources. The bottom 20 percent doesn't even get enough food to sustain basic life functions. As our country hoards the world's goods (and threatens the world with military destruction if they object), billions of people starve in misery and poverty around the world. "God is not pleased with this nation," Fr. Matthew concludes. "Not at all. One day there will be a great reckoning."

After Mass, I stand under the cold grey sky in the rain next to Merton's grave. "Help me to be faithful to Christ, to serve God, to be an apostle of nonviolence and peace, a servant of justice but a contemplative, too. Pray for me that these days may be blessed, that I may be pulled out of despair into new hope, that my heart may turn from a heart of stone to a heart of flesh, that a new spirit of compassion may awaken within me, and that I may do God's will. Intercede for me that I may become a faithful companion and disciple of Jesus."

When they are not working in the factory, doing their chores, or meditating in some quiet corner, the monks follow a rigorous schedule of psalm chanting and communal prayer in the Abbey church:

3:15 A.M. Vigils.
5:45 A.M. Laudes (6:45 on Sundays).
6:15 A.M. Mass (10:30 on Sundays).
7:15 A.M. Breakfast.
7:30 A.M. Terce (10:20 on Sundays).
12:15 P.M. Sext.
12:30 P.M. Dinner.
2:15 P.M. None.
5:30 P.M. Vespers.
6:00 P.M. Supper.
7:30 P.M. Compline.

I want to follow their rhythm of prayer during these next days.

I open to the Last Discourse of John's Gospel. "Whoever loves me will keep my word and my Father will love him and we will come to him and make our dwelling with him" (Jn 14:23). "I have told you this so that my joy might be in you and your joy might be complete" (Jn 15:11). "Remain in me as I remain in you" (Jn 15:14). The words sink in. I imagine and listen as Jesus whispers to me: "I am with you. I love you. Do not be afraid. Trust me. Stay with me. Everything will be all right. I want to share my joy with you." The words rise from a deep emptiness within me. An unusual peace settles upon me. I remain calm.

Later, I think about the half million refugees who have been fleeing Zaire in an endless single file line back into Rwanda and Burundi since Friday. So much human suffering in our world! Here I sit in silence. The best thing I can do for God and suffering humanity at this moment is to remain with God and listen and let God speak and let God's word soak in. I will trust God and God's word. God will tell me what to do, when to act, and where to go. God knows better than me. So I sit tight and hand over control to God.

Brother Patrick stops by my room with a gift, the page proofs of *Striving Towards Being,* a new volume of collected letters between Thomas Merton and Czeslaw Milosz, the Polish poet. The letters are filled with insight and wisdom. They challenge each other to remain hopeful in the face of the rock bottom despair of our times.

I head off to vespers. I get lost in my prayer booklet. I mix up the order of the psalms. Just as I find my place, the monks finish one psalm and move on to the next. Then the hunt through the prayer booklet begins again. I put the book down and listen to the praise of God. Glory upon glory.

Images, scenes, and faces from the Sacred Heart Center hover throughout the day, in prayer, during the office, on my walk. I see the faces of the countless neighborhood children: Kendrick, the nine-year-old fetal-alcohol syndrome boy who looks like a four year old, but who has the personality of a giant; the gentle smile of a shy first-grader named Erica; and the searching mind and kind-spirited second-grader Nelson, who told me one day, "I love it here." I spent so much time with administrative and fund-raising work that I hardly know these beautiful neighborhood people. I feel sad because my work kept me from better knowing these good, struggling people. Failure? I feel it in many ways, and yet I give thanks for the opportunity to serve there, to witness the hope of the people, to join in the many exciting programs and projects, and to know some generous, dedicated people.

After Compline, I attend the evening reflection offered by Fr. Matthew Kelty. He begins by reciting poems, including selections from Thomas More and Gerard Manley Hopkins. Then, the main talk. Tonight's topic: Forgiveness.

"There are three areas that require our forgiveness," he suggests. "First, we need to forgive God and to let go of the bitterness and umbrage we hold toward God for the suffering we see in the world. Once we accomplish that, we should move on and make love to God.

"Second, we must forgive our neighbors. Why? Because it's part of the contract: 'Forgive us our trespasses as we forgive. . . .'

"Third, we need to forgive ourselves and let go of guilt for our sins. This may be the most difficult of the three. If we cannot do this, or any other, then there is only one solution: Turn to the merciful Christ on the cross and ask him to forgive for us, through us, in us."

After a long pause, he concludes, "I'm sure he will grant your request."

I need to do all of these. I pray that the merciful, compassionate Christ will forgive me and give me the grace to forgive others—and to seek their forgiveness.

25

Later. Lying here on my bed, about to fall asleep, I realize what a remarkable day this has been. My spirit feels at ease, centered, at peace.

Thank you, Lord Jesus, for bringing me here. Please come and stay intimately close to me. Shower me with your merciful love, your consoling presence, your abiding love, and, in doing so, transform me. If there may be some way, allow me to serve you and your people with loving-kindness and compassion, and to announce your reign of love by radiating it with my life. Use me in your peacemaking work to resist the principalities and powers of systemic violence; to proclaim the truth of nonviolence; to follow you along the way of the cross so that your redemptive work can continue through me, absorbing the world's hatred violence and transforming it into mercy, reconciliation, and justice.

Lord, heal me, for I am broken and tired, restless and lost, bruised and hurt. I feel abandoned. I want to come home to you. Take me. Receive me. Grant me a new loving heart, a new inner peace, a life filled with joy, faith, hope, and love. Summon me to humble service and steadfast love toward others. May my life in you bear lasting fruit for humanity and all creation. Thank you for blessing me and the whole human family. I love you, O Christ. Amen.

Monday

After 3:15 A.M. Laudes and a tall cup of coffee, around 5:00 A.M. my meditation takes a second look at the people and places of the past years and gives thanks—for family and friends and work and gifts and blessings—for life itself! I pray for those whom I have hurt, and I request healing in that deep place within me where I have been wounded. I speak with Jesus in a quiet spirit of peace and confide my love for him. "I love you and am with you," my God tells me. "I have brought you here. I have carried you through all this. Stay with me and keep watch." These words offer a theme for my week.

Christ embraces me, holds me, and comforts me. "You are my beloved friend," he says. I long to live and remain in that loving embrace throughout eternity. It is the story of my life, the joy for which I was created, the reason for my hope and all I do, the good news I want to share with all. For what he says to me, he says to all. We are all his beloved friends.

And that means, praise God, we are all beloved friends of one another.

I set out on this new day filled with hope, renewed in God's love.

The hermitage: The little hermitage where Thomas Merton lived in the 1960s is farther away from the main monastery building than I thought. After vigils, Mass, and a visit with Brother Patrick, I proceed slowly, purposefully, mindfully, step by step, fully present, along the path, through the woods, up the gradual hill to the cottage. I am climbing up Mt. Zion, Mt. Tabor, Mt. Athos. I feel like Moses going up the mountain, so intense is the peace in my heart; the Spirit upon me. I give thanks and pray along the way. Approaching the hermitage, I come to the tall wooden cross, made from a paired down birch tree, and the simple wooden barrel wheel, leaning against it, rotting away after thirty-five years. With reverence, I kiss the cross. I am lost in the moment, the sanctity of the place, the energy of creation. Here is the cross of Christ, the cross of Merton, the cross of the church, the cross of nonviolence—my own cross. I enter the hermitage in silence. I take off my shoes. I kiss the ground.

I sit here in the holy silence of Thomas Merton's hermitage and feel a tremendous peace—a profound sense that I am on holy ground, in a holy place.

The hermitage is much simpler and poorer and smaller than I imagined. A white square structure with a flat roof, it has a large porch with three wooden beams supporting the overhanging roof. Along the wall under the front windows lies a row of logs, a wooden bench, and a wooden chair. Inside, the walls are exposed grey concrete blocks. The main rectangular room features a large stone fireplace, covered with black soot, in the center and three big windows looking out through the porch to the fields, trees, hills, and sky. A wooden table and chair sit before the window, with wicker rocking chairs on either side. A bookcase in the corner contains old copies of books by Merton and Merton's original volumes of the *Liturgy of the Divine Office* in Latin. John Howard Griffin's photograph of Merton, leaning over an open book, pen in hand, about to break into a smile, hangs in the corner. Also, by the front door there hangs an Asian Madonna and Child, painted on cloth and framed.

The door to the left of the fireplace leads back into the kitchen, which is compact and functional, with a sink, shelves, stove, cabinets, and a refrigerator. In the corner hangs the colorful calligraphy offering "the apostolic blessing" of Pope Paul VI to Thomas Merton. Over the sink hangs an old, hand-painted picture of "The Tree of Life," painted by a member of the Shaker community in the mid-1800s. Merton hung this painting here some thirty-five years ago.

To the right, beyond the kitchen, lies a small bedroom with a cot in the corner and an icon of the Nativity over it. To the left of the kitchen is the 1967 addition: two little rooms, a bathroom and a chapel. It is hard to imagine the great spiritual writer Merton living alone here for several years in the cold without a bathroom, walking out into the night to use an outhouse. The chapel is a small room with a pine wood altar (handmade by Merton's friend, Victor Hammer), a kneeler in front of it, a zazen in a corner, a tabernacle in the left corner behind it, and icons hanging on either side of a large wooden crucifix on the rear wall.

I sit in prayer and listen to the silence of Christ. "I have brought you here," he says happily, repeatedly. "I myself have done this."

A Transfiguration experience: Here atop Mt. Tabor, I see Christ transfigured, present, experienced in the profound silence and tangible holiness of this place. Like Moses, I approach the burning bush. Like Elijah, I feel the gentle breeze and hear the silent voice of God. Like Merton a few days before his accidental electrocution, I am transformed by the statues of Buddha in Polonnaruwa, Ceylon.

Every Christian needs a mountain where he or she can meet Christ. Here on this quiet mountain with Christ, I praise God and adore God in silent prayer. I enter the steadfast silence of the woods, the birds, the earth itself. The Great Listening of creation!

On the bookshelf, I discover *Follow the Ecstasy*, John Howard Griffin's biography of Merton's hermitage years. I imagine Merton alone here, at this desk, in this chapel, in this chair. I envision him here praying silently, meditating on the Gospels, writing poetry, chanting the psalms, looking out at the view, listening to the rain. I see him here with Joan Baez, sitting on the floor in front of the fire place. Or hosting a group of Hibakusha (survivors of the atomic blasts in Hiroshima and Nagasaki). Or making tea for Jacques Maritain. Or offering mass at the altar with Dan Berrigan. All the while staying close to Christ, centered in the Spirit of peace, rooted in the God of life. On this mountaintop, in the holy solitude and silence of the St. Mary of Mt. Carmel hermitage, I want to enter the intimate communion of love with Christ in the Spirit. I am present, alive, breathing, not doing anything else.

All is peace. With this visit, my life turns a corner. I hope now that I am entering some kind of spiritual adulthood, perhaps at last becoming a son of God, a disciple of Jesus, a contemplative, allowing my life to be given over to the Holy Spirit and not my own stubborn, disturbing will. The past year and a half's inner turbulence is healed in a moment by Christ's presence. I breathe again and face life and the future with new faith and confidence in the Spirit. And always, lurking in the back of my mind, that awesome fear—death. Perhaps I am being prepared even for death, because in the grace of this mountaintop experience, my fears are lifted. I can walk forward into life, into death and beyond to new life with hope.

> I come up the hill—
>   the fields green,
>   the sky grey,
>   the November trees—
> a homecoming.
> Holy, Holy, Holy,
> You stand on holy ground.
> The cottage—
> simple, poor, cold,
> grey concrete walls and floor,
> a fireplace,
> kitchen, bed, chapel—
> and a desk, looking out to the hills—
> there—
> the Spirit of Peace,
> Hope, at long last,
> calls me:
> Come,
> You are home.

The shock of being here is like a cold shower, a sudden realization, an epiphany. I'm reminded of those many mornings after the Plowshares disarmament action when I woke up to discover I was in jail. A bolt of lightning! A dose of reality. Here I experience the flip side—yes, a shock, a bolt of awareness. But here, on holy ground, where Merton lived and prayed and wrote, a taste of heaven on earth, the grace of solitude, the peace of silence, the joy of life. I intend to drink the cup all the way to the bottom.

The monks have filled the refrigerator with cheese, eggs, fruitcake, apple juice, and bottled water. I've been sitting here in the front room all morning, looking out the window, taking it all in—the silence, the view, the aura, the poverty and simplicity of the place, the goodness. At long last, a house of peace.

The hours go by in complete silence, stillness. So this is solitude! I have never known it so completely. I recall receiving permission from my Jesuit superiors to live by myself, write, and house-sit in our "Casa San Jose" community house during my theology studies in the summers of 1990 and 1991, in a low-income neighborhood in Oakland, California. I was all alone for three months each summer. What a revelation! All my inner demons came to the surface. I struggled to make peace with myself. They were days of great pain, as well as deep inner joy. My spirit swung from despair to rapture, from anguish to freedom. A great experience of self-discovery.

Here, nothing. Trees, fields, rain. A place where time stands still, a place of no time, a place beyond time, a place where the Spirit lives. Now I know and experience what Merton wrote in his autobiographical essay, "Day of a Stranger."

> What I wear is pants.
> What I do is live.
> How I pray is breathe. . . .
> Up here in the woods is seen the New Testament.

That is to say, the wind comes through the trees and you breathe it.

I have not brought my word processor. I have no books except the Bible. I left behind my address book and do not write any letters. There is no phone, no TV, no radio, no newspaper, no mail, no fax machine—nothing but the silence.

What do you do if you find yourself on Mount Tabor? You fall down in worship and adoration. You heed the voice in the clouds which says convincingly, "Listen!" What I hear—the silence of God, the contemplation of heaven, the peace of the communion of saints—is more profound than any book.

At this table, Merton wrote "Blessed are the Meek," one of the best reflections ever written on Christian nonviolence. Here he lived it and received Jesus' blessing. He inherited the earth, the vision outside the window. I do not know how to enter into that same inheritance, but I have come here to listen, to begin anew, to try, to pray, to receive that meekness, that blessing.

Who am I that I should receive this grace? It is a big joke. This does not make me better, holier, worthier than anyone else. I take a deep breath and give thanks to You for bringing me here, for granting me this taste of heaven. I take heart and pray that I make the best of it, that I use this week wisely to give praise and lift up the entire human race and its every need to our Lord and Savior, Jesus, and to God, the Creator. Yes, I will simply be present here. I feel I am coming alive after a long sleep, almost for the first time.

Merton's account of his experience before the great stone Buddhas at Polonnaruwa in Ceylon just before he died characterizes the way I feel right now. I pick up a copy of *The Asian Journal.* He describes them as

> filled with every possibility, questioning nothing, knowing everything, rejecting nothing, the peace not of emotional resignation but of Madhyamika, of sunyata, that has seen through every question without trying to discredit anyone or anything—without refutation—without establishing some other argument. For the doctrinaire, the mind that needs well-established positions, such peace, such silence, can be frightening. . . . [I am] suddenly, almost forcibly, jerked clean out of the habitual, half-tied vision of things, and an inner clearness, clarity becomes evident, obvious. . . . All matter, all life, is charged with dharmakaya. . . . Everything is emptiness and everything is compassion.

There is no way I can will such an experience. It comes as pure gift. I can only receive it with gratitude. I bow down here after seven years of climbing and give thanks that I have reached this peak—maybe not the top, of course, but a clear resting place where I can catch my breath and regain my spirit for the final journey up and beyond into the clouds and the Great Spirit.

Merton's journal from the hermitage, 1964–65, *A Vow of Conversation,* records his initial days alone in the woods and the peace and beauty he received:

In the hermitage I see how quickly one can fall apart. I talk to myself, I dance around the hermitage, I sing. This is all very well, but it is not serious. (December 4, 1964)

In the hermitage, one must pray or go to seed. The pretense of prayer will not suffice. Just sitting will not suffice. It has to be real. Yet, what can one do? Solitude puts you with your back to the wall, or your face to it, and this is good. So you pray to learn how to pray. (December 5, 1964)

In solitude everything has its weight for good or for evil and one must attend carefully to everything. If you apply yourself carefully to what you do, great springs of strength and truth are released in you. (December 7, 1964)

The rain on the roof accentuates the silence and surrounds the dryness and light of the hermitage as though with love and peace. The liberty and tranquility of this place are indescribable, more than any bodily peace. This is a gift of God marked with God's simplicity and God's purity. How one's heart opens and what hope arises in the core of my being! It is as if I had not really hoped in God for years, as if I had been living all this time in despair. (December 11, 1964)

These words echo my experience here, now, today. And again:

The great joy of the solitary life is not found simply in quiet, in the beauty and peace of nature or in the song of birds or even in the peace of one's own heart. It resides in the awakening and the attuning of the inmost heart to the voice of God—to the inexplicable, quiet, definite inner certitude of one's call to obey God, to hear God, to worship God, here, now, today in silence and alone. (June 8th, 1965)

After his first week living here full time, he writes:

The five days I have had in real solitude have been a revelation. . . . It is a life of peace, silence, purpose and meaning. (August 25, 1965)

Over the past years, I have roamed around, restless. Yet today, all my demons, anxieties, fears, and hostilities are exorcized, and my true inner self—for a moment at least!—shines through. At long last! A return to innocence, truth, grace, being, poverty of self; the feeling of the hand of God resting gently upon me, just by my being here. (But I do not want to fall into the deadly spiritual trap of thinking that somehow I have done something to deserve this or am no longer a sinner! I must remember who I am!)

The eschatology of the place. It is as if the Son of Humanity will be coming in over the clouds and hills any minute. And very well he might. The reading at Mass from Luke: "Gird your loins, light your lamp, stay awake and keep watch. You know not the hour. . . ."

Merton spent time here preparing for his death, which he sensed was coming soon. Perhaps these recent graces are preparing me for my coming death. I pray that I may be ready. I want to be found faithful, loving, peaceful, forgiving, and accepting. I pray for the gift of a peaceful, blessed death.

Matthew Kelty preached a few lines at morning Mass. "In the past, when the trains passed by in the night," he said, "you could hear the clickity-clack sound of the train passing over the tracks. But now, as the tracks get smoother, you don't hear that anymore. Life is like that. Our paths smooth out as we grow older. And death is okay. We are not created to travel. We are meant to arrive."

"Gird your loins and light your lamps," Jesus instructs his disciples urgently. "Be like servants who await their master's return from a wedding, ready to open the door immediately when he comes and knocks. Blessed are those servants who the master finds vigilant on his arrival. Amen, he will gird himself, have them recline at table, and proceed to wait on them. And should he come in the second or third watch and find them prepared in this way, blessed are those servants. . . . You must be prepared, for at an hour you do not expect, the Son of Humanity will come" (Lk 12:35–40).

For an hour, I stay with this instruction and pray to be prepared for Christ's arrival, to be ready, alert, awake, and found faithful. I remember that what follows in the text is the scene at Gethsemani, where the disciples fall asleep, and Jesus, alone and in the anguish of prayer, remains awake. When the imperial troops arrive, only he remains nonviolent and fearless. The disciples strike out in violence, cut off one soldier's ear, and flee. Mark calls us to remain awake, detached from all competing ideological sides of violence. We are summoned to be "neither victim nor victimizer," but practitioners of revolutionary, contemplative nonviolence, like Jesus, who speak the truth with love until the authorities arrest us and haul us away.

I imagine sitting in this living room with Jesus, and beside him, Merton and Dorothy Day. They look intently at me. Then together we look at Christ and listen attentively to him. His company feels so close, so real, so consoling.

Merton would hate such prayer and call it idolatrous, but to me, it is quintessential Ignatian spirituality and real to my spirit. Someday, the scene will be actual: I will be with them.

I pray for the human family. Right now, while the hawks and the crows circle above in the sky and the rain quietly falls, I bask in communion with Christ. I ask for blessings on creation and the whole human race—an end to all wars, all injustices, all violence, racism, sexism, the death penalty, abortion, hunger, prisons, AIDS, cancer, torture, hatred, consumerism; for the dismantling of all nuclear weapons, bombs, Trident submarines, destroyers, bombers, and guns; for the coming of God's reign of nonviolence and love; for the conversion of hearts; for a new reconciling spirit among God's people around the world. Come Lord Jesus. Delay no longer.

Later. After a long walk, I cross the field and approach the hermitage. Suddenly, seven gun shots ring out close by in the woods to the right of the hermitage. I nearly faint. A hunter! "Well, if I get shot," I think, "this is a good place to die. What a grace and a blessing to die here at the monastery, at the hermitage." I keep walking.

After taking a nap, I see the hunter's truck parked in the field and go out to speak with him. He approaches me carrying a huge rifle across his shoulder. "I'll try not to shoot you," he says. Stunned, I thank him. He tells me he has been hunting around here since the 1960s. I am appalled. "Well, as I say, I'll try not to shoot you," he repeats as he walks away. I stare back in disbelief.

I had been thinking of death all day long. In recent years, I have feared death with nothing but sheer terror. I have seen bombings and war in El Salvador, Israel, Nicaragua,

Guatemala, and the Philippines, but turbulent airplane flights have shaken me up even more. But this afternoon, as I rest under the icon of the Nativity on Merton's bed (a cot with a firm mattress, supported by plywood), death feels like the most natural thing in the world. Everyone dies. Everyone goes there, wherever *there* is. It must surpass even this serenity because I will be with Christ and all the saints. It will be peaceful and joyful, like a great wedding banquet. Indeed, the harder challenge is to remain here and carry out the Gospel's urgent mission to resist the forces of death, to oppose death's warmaking power, to risk my life making life more liveable for others.

Now that I've faced the hunter—who will *try* not to shoot me (no guarantees, mind you)—my fervor subsides. The euphoria has cooled down. It's late (5:00 P.M.) and nearly dark as I write this, and I'm tired.

It is a miracle of grace to be here and rest in the peace of Christ. Being here is far better than any conference or seminar on peace or prayer could ever be. Here, I come to terms with myself. I face my soul and plumb my inner depths and pass beyond my inner turbulence. I encounter the Holy. The peace and solitude of this hermitage and the spirit of its founder teach me how to be at peace. My roots sink deeper into the Spirit. I hope and trust that as my roots go deeper, my life will bear good fruit for God's greater glory. I pray that the peace I experience here will disarm me and make me into a true instrument of Christ's peace.

I light candles and place them on the altar in the little chapel. I sit on the stool facing the altar, the crucifix, the icons, and the tabernacle, and read John's resurrection account. "The disciples rejoiced when they saw the Lord," I read (Jn 20:20). I feel like rejoicing. All the anxiety, fear, and insecurities which I have carried around these past years have been lifted, through no effort of my own. I sit with the Lord. "You are my friend," he says quietly. "I give you my peace. Stay with me."

Such moments of faith are deeply consoling. I wish they would last throughout my life, or at least, that I would not forget them so quickly.

Yes, I have been carrying many burdens. As I think of them, I am not at all surprised that I have been so depressed. The Sacred Heart Center, its exhausting fundraising needs, management problems, personnel difficulties, the grant-writing and maintenance work, plus the talks and liturgies and meetings; before that, eight months in jail for Gospel peacemaking; on top of this, several broken relationships; a Jesuit friend's departure from the Society; the absence of community; and throughout it all, a string of deaths this past year—from my uncle, John Regan, to my friends, Ruth Payne, Mev Puleo, Marty Jenco, Ray Donovan, Debbie Reeves, and now most recently, Henri Nouwen. It has been a difficult year. My spirit has been beaten down. I pray that the Lord may renew me and give me a new heart, new hope, permanent peace, and his own lasting joy. For once, I would like to learn from these painful experiences and grow—spiritually, emotionally, humanly—to become finally more compassionate, more trusting, more hopeful. That will require the grace of God, taking time for myself, and long hours of silent, healing, intimate prayer.

That is the point of my presence here, to plunge into the solitude and silence of God. This is not an ego trip, a tourist stop, or a research project. My very soul is at stake. Communion with Christ is the purpose of this journey. So hard to explain this to others—and to myself.

Sitting in the chapel again, with the candle lit, giving thanks, enjoying Christ's peace, friendship, fellowship, and company. I could stay here forever. In the most recently published Merton journal, *Turning Toward the World*, Merton confesses his one and only wish: to die in this hermitage. I understand his desire. The silence is heavenly.

I stand on the porch. All is quiet. This place, this silent, holy night, is like a perpetual Advent, an ongoing Easter.

I look up to the half moon. I thank God for this glorious day and call to the saints to pray for me and to the Lord in his mercy to bless me. He already has, mightily.

I hope I never forget the graces of this day, and that they deepen my trust, faith, and friendship in Christ, who has made it possible, who has graciously given it to me. I fall asleep, tired but excited, amazed and content, and finally, for the first time in years, deeply consoled.

Tuesday

As the deer longs for running water
so my soul longs for you, O God.
My soul thirsts for God, the living God.
When shall I go and behold the face of God? . . .
Deep calls unto deep. . . .
By day, the Lord bestows his grace;
at night I have his song,
a prayer to my living God. . . .
I sing to God my rock.

—Ps 42

A night of peace and tranquility in these Kentucky woods. I rest calmly beneath Merton's Nativity icon. I feel watched over, ministered to by the angels themselves, as our Lord in the wilderness.

Up by 4:30 A.M., I clean up, bundle up—it is very cold now—and follow the spotlight of my flashlight through the pitch black night down to the monastery for vigils and Mass.

Then, I indulge in coffee and a long visit with Brother Patrick in the new community dining room. He tells me of his life, from Notre Dame to Gethsemani, his friends, his work on Merton's writing, the hermitage. He is good and kind to me and exemplifies St. Benedict's spirit of monastic hospitality. Afterwards, I chat with Carlos, the Filipino priest whom I first met in 1989. He exudes life and love for all people; he is interested in everything. Then, I reach my mother by phone. On Sunday, my father came home from the hospital. He feels much better. The leg infection has healed dramatically, but he is weak after a week in the hospital. I told her I would return home when my retreat ends. She comments that many angels must be keeping watch over him.

The sun tries to come out. It is a true November morning—cold and grey, with hints of blue and white light in the sky, a haze in the distance over the hills and trees, the ground covered with wet leaves, the trees dead and barren except for the pines. Merton probably planted these pines long ago.

I sit content, held in the peace of Christ, as if God herself is embracing me. The silence is magnificent and healing. I become part of it—silent, calm, at peace. My soul is quieted.

This place reminds me of the one-room cottage built for Daniel Berrigan by theologian William Stringfellow on Block Island, Rhode Island—the square cottage with a desk, books, table, kitchen, and a small bedroom featuring a wall of photos (including Merton's). Dan is there now, and I can imagine him fixing coffee, praying, writing his latest biblical study—this one on Samuel and the book of Kings—and cooking up a gourmet feast for island friends. The cottage stands atop a cliff overlooking the ocean on holy ground. Stringfellow lies buried there in a cluster of pine trees near a pond.

I think, too, of the glorious seventy-fifth birthday party we threw for Dan last May at St. Francis Xavier Church social hall in New York City. Nearly seven hundred people attended. A long table of homemade gourmet food was served by an array of volunteers. Liam Neeson offered a toast. Allen Ginsberg read poetry. Phil Berrigan, Elizabeth McAlister, and others offered tributes. But the highlight came when Pete Seeger took the stage with his banjo. He led us in a long, slow rendition of "Where Have All the Flowers Gone?"

Later, a long-time activist from a non-religious anti-war organization wrote with amazement and wonder at the loving spirit that pervaded the hall throughout the evening. "See how these Christians love one another!" he wrote. "Perhaps they're not so bad after all."

I write at Merton's old wooden desk. I look out the window at the dawn. I breathe in and soak up the peace of the moment, a glimpse of God's reign. Here I feel the peace of resurrection. I drink the living water flowing from Christ's heart. Jesus shows me his hands and his side and whispers "Shalom" the word on the plaque by the front door. Here, like the apostles in heaven, I rejoice, for I know my redeemer lives. I know my Savior rules. I believe I shall see my God in the land of the living.

I will remain in this spirit of hope and resurrection. More importantly, I will enter into the experience of Christ in my own heart and let him touch me and live in me and breathe his spirit of peace and love upon me. I realize again that Christ indeed is my hope, my peace, my salvation. I offer him my desires and burdens and weaknesses. I hand over to him my family and friends, my community, and the human race. I fall at his feet in love and adoration, and I offer myself to his mercy.

I am blessed. And although I am not worthy of one of these blessings, I will not hide it. God is good to me. For a moment before the sun rises, I realize it. God blesses me. Praise God, then. All glory to God.

This desk—
plain, brown, wood,
not so beautiful—
has seen its share of life—
essays against war,
books on prayer,
letters writ large with love—
and tears too,
but most of all,
soul—
hidden, open
in early morning light—
one long prayer
to the One who is.

The cold cell of Merton's bedroom brings back memories of the Chowan County Jail cell where I spent six long months with Phil Berrigan and Bruce Friedrich after our Plowshares anti-nuclear disarmament action at the Seymour Johnson Air force Base on December 7, 1993. At night in the winter, the concrete walls felt like a meat storage refrigerator. How long and hard those days were, filled with much despair and yet moments of great consolation, especially in our daily Bible studies and simple Eucharists. Here now, in the cold with a fire burning, I feel new hope, consolation, and immense gratitude for those awesome days.

I think again of the good people and difficult work of the Sacred Heart Center. As one of the Jesuit Volunteer

Corps community members commented, it is a place of "chaotic grace." Everyday, amidst great confusion, crises, and excitement, we struggled to keep it afloat and, because of tremendous blessings, kept paddling forward. For me personally, the center entailed terrible pressures. I did not have much previous experience with administrative work, personnel management, and fundraising obligations, and difficulties with one of my coworkers compounded the situation. My provincial has reassigned me now. No Jesuit is available to replace me as Director, but the center will grow even stronger under the leadership of a young woman, a Catholic social worker.

All that is past. Grace heals all the wounds. I mourn the pain and death involved in this experience, but I feel the gift of new life beckoning me and I send all my blessings to the Sacred Heart Center and my former coworkers there. Most of all, I call blessings upon the children and women from the countless low-income neighborhood families, struggling to survive the nightmare of poverty and violence, that God might give them every chance of life and peace.

I look out at the world—
trees, hills, sky,
the birds of the air,
the fields, the breeze—
and see—
not war,
not pain,
not sorrow,
not the brutal 9 to 5
which kills spirit and soul—
but for once,

for all—
Peace.

O God, You are my hope and my refuge. You are my strength. You are the source of life itself. You are love and peace and truth. You are, as Merton wrote, "Mercy within Mercy within Mercy." You are nonviolent and compassionate, ever gentle to all your children. Have pity on each one of us, on every member of the human race. We have ruined your world, despised your gifts, rejected your love, disdained your kindness. We do not know what we are doing. Forgive us. We are blind, sinful, stupid, mean, and arrogant. We kill one another, treat each other unjustly, and destroy your earth.

We do not know what we are doing. We are like drunkards on a rampage, out of our minds.

Come, help us become sober. Put a spirit of repentance in our hearts. Give us a change of heart. Let this generation wake up from our nightmare of sin, of violence. Help us to reconcile with one another, disarm our weapons, feed the hungry, house the homeless, liberate the imprisoned, heal the sick, respect all people, love one another, forgive ourselves, and learn finally to live in peace with You and each other.

We can never learn your wisdom on our own. Do not leave us to ourselves. We are, as Merton would say, "insane." We wish to be made whole and to celebrate your glory with praise and thanksgiving. Please, take pity on us. You are our only hope.

Here Thomas read Julian
and learned her prayer
 through a bitter cold night
long as war:

"All will be well,
all will be well, and
all manner of things
will be
well."

Outside, I see blue jays, crows, squirrels, and a fat wood-chuck. Other than that, nothing moves. Everything stands still, frozen in time, as if Earth itself were at prayer, on retreat. I expect the hills to start singing any moment.

Later (10:30 A.M.). The sun is out and shining for the first time in days. The fire in the wood-burning heater begins to warm the room. I read *The Book of the Poor in Spirit,* which was written in the fourteenth century by an anonymous Dominican, who signed himself, "A Friend of God." The book was recommended to Merton by his English friend Etta Gulick (according to *The Hidden Ground of Love: Letters*), and he relished it. The way to God, according to this mystic, is found in peace of heart, detachment, freedom, grace, suffering, contemplative listening, and discipleship to Christ. In solitude, these states appear not only as goals worth striving for, but as eminently reachable.

12:30 P.M. Reading favorite books borrowed from the guesthouse library—Dan Berrigan's *Portraits of Those I Love;* Henri Nouwen's *The Return of the Prodigal Son;* Louis Fisher's *The Life of Mahatma Gandhi; The Prison Meditations of Alfred Delp, S.J.*; and Merton's *The Behavior of Titans.* It is warm outside now and bright, though still overcast. I write while seated on a bench on the front porch of the hermitage, after having taken a walk along the paths through the woods and into the fields surrounding the house. In the distance, the bells toll. Sext prayers are being offered. The birds sing.

A crow cries out. I keep watch, keep faith, read my Bible, say my prayers. I am on the lookout, so to speak, for Christ, coming to me any moment.

My soul is set in peace, O God, and awaits your coming. Have mercy on me, your unworthy servant, your friend. Delay no longer.

> I close my eyes and take a breath.
> See!
> All around—
> trees, hills, birds, sky—
> radiate,
> sing Your praise,
> a new heaven,
> a new earth—
> O bless the Lord, my soul—
> at long last come.

Thomas Merton writes at the end of one of his first letters to Czeslaw Milosz (February 28, 1959):

> Life is on our side. The silence and the Cross of which we know are forces that cannot be defeated. In silence and suffering, in the heartbreaking effort to be honest in the midst of dishonesty (most of all our dishonesty), in all these is victory. It is Christ in us who drives us through darkness to a light of which we have no conception and which can only be found by passing through apparent despair. Everything has to be tested. All relationships have to be tried. All loyalties have to pass through fire. Much has to be lost. Much in us has to be killed, even much that is best in us. But victory is certain. The Resurrection is the only light, and with that light, there is no error.

The birch cross stands close by, maybe ten yards away. Merton spent hours resting and reading here, "in the shadow of this cross." It symbolizes everything. Here we place our hopes and dreams, not in the way of violence or power or domination, not in the snares and traps of the world, the world's lies and temptations to success and efficacy; but in the cross, the way of nonviolence, peaceful resistance to evil, suffering love in the face of injustice, truth-telling in a world of lies, powerlessness as a way to unhinge empires. In this cross is the resurrection. For it stands barren, empty, a sign of Christ's victory over death. The empire does not have the final say. Life does not conclude with an abyss of suffering. It becomes transformed, transfigured, into glory, the new life at God's banquet table, in God's house of peace and love. This cross is silent, but through the centuries it affirms our ultimate hope: *Life is on our side!* God is a God of life, not death, and we too shall enter that reign of life.

The Jesus I meet on Merton's porch is risen. All around me I hear his testimony: "I am the Resurrection and the Life. I am the Way, the Truth and the Life."

The bells of Gethsemani ring out. "Hear them, John: they call you home."

The cross stands
after all these years—
weathered,
rugged,
a witness to the Way,
tried by few—
the Way of pain,
of Love—tried, true.

It blends in with the woods,
and could be mistaken
for a tree.
But it is all the difference
between life and death;
marks this house,
this land, this earth;
bespeaks Christ
who died, rose,
and sets us free.
It stands—
witness
in a world of war
and speaks
of peace:
"Forgive, all, now;
Put away your sword;
Love one another.
Your Liberation is at hand."

I have been sitting on this porch in silence for over an hour (1–2 P.M.). I have done nothing, produced nothing, accomplished nothing. I have barely moved a muscle.

There are moments when I feel like Buddha, sitting under his tree. Silence breaks through judgment and self-righteousness and false certainties, into the present moment. Once you realize the power of reality, you wish never again to waste a minute in mindlessness. This represents the new spirit of life promised with Christ's resurrection.

I listen to the words of Christ: "Come to me, all you who labor and are burdened, and I will give you rest. . . . Learn from me, for I am meek and humble of heart, and you will find rest for yourselves" (Mt 11:28–30). Christ speaks these words to me. He calls me and holds me. At one point, I imagine him in white robes, walking across the field, on these grounds, up to this porch, standing before me, at one with the peace and silence. Afterwards, I mutter under my breath, without realizing it, "Holy, Holy, Holy." This goes on and on. I name him—the Christ of nonviolence, the Christ of peace, the Christ of compassion, the Christ of justice. I enter, at his invitation, his solitude. The world is transfigured.

Holy, holy, holy. Worthy is the Lamb who was slain. Holy, holy, holy. Behold the Lamb of God who takes away the sins of the world. Holy, holy, holy, the One who is our peace. Blessed are we.

Returning from a walk, I meet Father Paschal and two workmen as they arrive to install a new intercom system between the hermitage and the Abbey, "in case you have a heart attack and need help," he says with a smile. Apparently, that just happened recently to a Trappist hermit in Oregon. Just before he lost consciousness, he paged the monastery on his intercom. The brothers ran to the hermitage. An ambulance was called. He survived. Upon hearing the story, the Abbot ordered intercoms installed in all four of Gethsemani's hermitages.

As I walk the fields, I think about yesterday's encounter with the hunter. I recall facing death squads in El Salvador, war in Israel and Nicaragua, street violence in Washington, D.C., and New York city, jail, even a personal death threat by the insane parent of one of my Scranton, Pennsylvania, high school students. But I never dreamed of gunshots at Gethsemani! It is appalling that hunting occurs here (or anywhere!), that someone stalks these monastic woods with a rifle, ready to kill. The world at Merton's door, at my door.

Violence is everywhere. There is no getting away from it. But I carry on, trying to live the quiet wisdom of nonviolence.

Here at the hermitage I undertake that "ontology of nonviolence" which Merton called for in the closing line of his book, *Mystics and Zen Masters.* I pondered it seven years ago when I first came here, but this hermitage invites me deeper into Buddha's enlightenment, that deep presence, freedom, detachment, and pure peace which is untouched by fear, anxiety, or violence. I am exhilarated. I find myself whole or, more accurately, I realize in the flash of the moment the possibility of inner wholeness. The challenge will be to live out this state of grace—to walk into the world faithful to the peace I have received. This will require that I confront the violence around me, but not in a spirit of retaliation. As Cesar Chavez once said to me, it's easy for monks and hermits to be nonviolent. The real test comes with public action on the picket lines. I know I must face those lines again. I pray for a heart of ontological nonviolence.

I pick up the aging pre-Vatican II Mass Missal and Sacramentary, all in Latin! Merton used it in the chapel when he was finally permitted to offer Mass here. I read and translate the Latin words of consecration. Though I was an altar boy at many morning Latin Masses, I still do not grasp the drastic liturgical changes which the church has undergone. A Latin Mass is unimaginable to me now. It comes from another world. I can not relate the experience of those who labored and suffered in the "old" church to my experience growing up in the Vatican II church "of the people." I thank God for these changes and pray for more. The old church is dying and, like this Latin book, will be shelved. A new church is being born, engendered by the Spirit. It is Christ who leads the church into the future. And so I pray for the clergy's right to marriage, for the ordination of women as priests, for a spirit of democracy and collegiality within the global Roman Catholic community and its leadership, and most of all, for its full conversion to the way of nonviolence, its active resistance to greed, war, and nuclear weapons, and its complete commitment to Gospel peacemaking.

The fire burns in the fireplace, but smoke lingers in the room. I'm sure the chute is open, but something must be wrong. It's a lively fire and it keeps me warm, so I don't mind the smoke. Let it be like incense.

> Here I speak with the dead.
> We visit and sip tea.
> We read, we write, we pray.
> Tom, Dorothy, Martin, Gandhi.
> They smile,
> look into my eyes,
> like Christ,
> sparkling, alight, aglow.
> We live, we are not dead.
> *Long Live Life!*

Your solitude will bear immense fruit in the souls of men and women you will never see on earth.

—God to Merton, at the end of
The Seven Storey Mountain

7 P.M. A visitation. Father Paschal sent word that I was having difficulty with the fireplace and the wood-burning heater. Brother Anthony arrives in the pickup truck. He discovers that the flue in the chimney is not open all the way, fixes it, climbs up on the roof, sweeps out the chimneys, then shows me how to build a fire in the wood-burning heater (kindling wood, paper, kerosene, then lastly, once the fire is roaring, the logs). The smoke clears up and the room warms.

As he finishes, I inquire about his life. He talks for an hour and a half. After attending college in his home state of Nebraska, he suffered a serious motorcycle accident. During his recovery, he read the lives of the saints. While pondering the life of John of the Cross, he experienced a spiritual awakening. Eventually, he entered a nearby monastery for four months. Feeling not quite at home, he wrote to Gethsemani, came for a visit, and stayed. That was July, 1968. After his novitiate, in 1970, he made a silent week-long retreat here. Eight years ago, he was appointed the custodian of the Merton hermitage. He checks on guests and keeps the place going. Short, thin, young-looking, he's been a monk for twenty-eight years.

As one of the main factory cooks, he spends long hours at the stove each day, so he does not go to the offices, except for vigils and Mass in the morning. Five years ago, he started studying Zen, and now it's his main interest. The Buddhist vow of compassion for all living things has been the key to his spirituality.

As he fixes the fire, I ask him if he has any advice. I think in terms of operating the wood-burning heater. He presumes I refer to my spiritual life.

"I have a Zen koan for you to ponder," he says turning to me. *"What is the sound of listening?"*

He pauses and looks at me intently. The fire crackles. The sound of listening?

"We are born into listening," he observes, "and we die into listening. Spend every minute here at the hermitage, like Merton, listening for the Spirit, letting the Spirit breathe in you and come alive in you. That's what prayer is about. You need no books, nothing at all. Just sit. Breathe in. Breathe out. And listen.

"It is that simple.

"Dan Walsh, Merton's teacher who lived here towards the end of his life, was a great help to me in the 1970s," he continues. "He explained to us Merton's teaching about the true self and the false self, and how each one of us needs to go deep within, into our true selves, to break through the fear and violence of our false selves which constrict us. We need to go beyond knowledge and thought into Mystery, into the Beyond, into God, to become Love, to become lost in Love, in the Divine, into a new consciousness. We find our the true selves through total inner transformation."

I remember the concluding words of Merton's last talk, given just hours before he died, at the monastic conference in Bangkok on December 10, 1968. Merton called his listeners to the task of "total inner transformation."

I ask about Christ. Brother Anthony pauses.

"Christ is the perfect human," he muses, "the transparent reflection of Being, of God, who shows us ourselves. The point is to enter into the Mystery, into union with perfect being, God, to become Christ. Ultimately, each one of us is Christ. We need to break through our fears, our traps, and just be peace, and listen. Then, we become our true selves. We become who we already are. We become the Christ already within us. What we need is great faith," he concludes, "to enter into Being, to feel compassion for all, and to realize true peace."

I'm overwhelmed by his lecture, and I want now to sit and be and breathe and listen and dwell in the Spirit of Christ, the Spirit of peace, to journey toward the "total inner transformation" of my soul into God.

Night has fallen. Silence has come upon me again. I sit and close my eyes and breathe. I feel at one with everyone, and thus, with Christ, with God.

For an hour, I sit in peace, in Buddhist mindfulness, attentive to my breathing, my being. It's 8:20 P.M. now, and I'm enjoying some Trappist cheese with crackers and bottled water and write at Merton's desk. I love that way of prayer and have for over ten years, and the monk only pushes me to go deeper into the Spirit of prayer. But I want Christ, too! I want Buddhist mindfulness and Zen goodness and Ignatian contemplation all rolled into one! And, I believe, I am being given it! That is what is so extraordinary about all the blessings I have received—from peacemaking and Gospel nonviolence, to voluntary poverty and public witness, to solidarity with the poor and imprisonment for disarmament. I have been called to plunge the depths of prayer from day one, the day of my conversion, Ash Wednesday, 1980, when I decided, in my fraternity room at Duke University, in a moment to grace, to accept faith in Christ and offer up my life as a Jesuit priest. Ever since, I've been trying to go deeper into that mystical reality. I stray frequently, but the quest is the essence of my life. I want to join the mystical together with the public, prophetic, compassionate, nonviolent work for justice and peace. I seek to combine the mystic's calling and the prophet's calling and the saint's calling and the apostle's calling, like Jesus did.

It's 9 P.M. A stick of Japanese Jasmin incense burns slowly on the mantle while I read Milosz and Merton. It is quiet again with only an occasional crackle or pop from the wood-burning heater. I will turn in now, but I want to record my amazement and gratitude for this glorious day of peace to God, to the living Christ, and to my patron, Thomas Merton. A great gift. I bless God and give thanks. Amen.

Wednesday

The sun is shining, and the sky is clear blue, a magnificent November morning. A white frost covers the grass, and a hazy mist hovers over the trees on distant hills.

This morning when I went up to the monastery (at 5:30 A.M.) for Mass followed by coffee with Brother Patrick, the stars were out. I have not seen that many stars in years. You cannot see the stars in New York City or Richmond or Washington, D.C. But here in the woods, heaven shows her face.

The Trappist feast, "For All Deceased Superiors of the Orders," was celebrated at Mass today and included a reading from the Passion. The words of the repentant thief linger: "Jesus, remember me, when you come into your kingdom." They are my words. Coming here, feeling hurt, bruised, and battered, I say them and repeat them. Here in this hermitage, looking out at these hills with the sun pouring through the window and fire roaring away in the heater, in this solitude, Jesus responds, "Today, you shall be with me in paradise."

These cold concrete walls remind me of jail. The charcoal smell and the fire remind me of the Calle Real refugee camp in El Salvador, where I lived for awhile in 1985. (Though it was summer, fires were kept burning all the time, for cooking during the day and warmth in the evening.) The peace and tranquility remind me of Block Island, Rhode Island. "Today you will be with me in paradise." Jesus has brought me here and shared this paradise with me. I offer silent thanks and praise.

All night, thinking of Brother Anthony's sermon on Zen, I said to myself, *Yes*, I want that. I want to live in that deep centered inner space. But all that centering is merely preparation, for I want to enter into the presence of Christ, to worship Christ, my brother and Lord.

For me, prayer is adoration of my Lord and Savior. Prayer is living worship. It is loving God in Christ, with my whole heart, soul, mind, and spirit. Zen helps me with that latter part, but the focus is on God. I know this because I have experienced a personal God over the years. I have been touched by an other-worldly, unconditional, still-unimaginable, never-ending Love which is the Creator, the Christ, and the Spirit. I think of Christ's response to the temptations in the desert, especially the third: "You shall worship God; God alone shall you adore." That is what I try to do in my own inner life.

Through the graces of Merton's hermitage and the kindness of Brother Patrick and the community, I am able to do just that. I plunge the depths of my desire. My worship is fulfilled. I am granted access. I am allowed to approach the

Holy. I feel like Moses on the mountain. Leaving here will mean coming down from the mountaintop. I do not want to leave, but I know that I must, for I still have a mission—the commandments of nonviolence to proclaim, the waters of imperial violence to part, an exodus to accompany, a pillar of fire to uphold, bread in the wilderness to offer.

I am not equating myself with Moses. This is not arrogance, but an image for understanding my journey. This is the common vocation of all Christians—to make the biblical stories of our ancestors, from Moses through the prophets to Jesus, our own story. I'm trying to do that with my own life and trying to understand my encounter with God in the spirit of peace here at Merton's hermitage. These are important days in my life, days of grace and blessing, and I want to remember them and understand their meaning.

Up here, there are no questions, no answers, and for the first time in a long time, no problems. There is only presence, adoration of Christ, worship of God. There is only Life itself—living it, breathing it, drinking the cup of the present moment to the bottom. This cup is the cup of compassion, peace, and love.

I do not deny the world. My heart is filled with the faces of poverty, from the children of the Sacred Heart Center, to El Salvador, to Haiti, to friends in jail, to places I have never visited—Rwanda, the Sudan, Peru, Bosnia, East Timor, Calcutta. I think of the unborn, those on death row, those dying of cancer and AIDS, the imprisoned and homeless and hungry, as well as those working in the military, all the millions of people around the world who are killing one another, preparing to kill one another in war, or maintaining weapons of death. I come here with the whole human race in mind. My being here is a prayer for the world, a plea for peace and compassion. Despite my own poverty and weakness, I feel my prayer is heard by God and accepted. It is a mystery, my contribution to the intercessory contemplative work of the church. It is an easy burden, a light yoke, and I rejoice in these days of silence and peace. May they bear fruit, in Christ's name.

I sit perfectly still in Merton's rocking chair, worshiping Christ, mindfully breathing in and out, looking out at the view. Jesus, remember me when you come into your kingdom, I whisper. "John, I myself have brought you here to share with you my paradise," he replies. I see his hands, his wounds, his eyes, his smile. I feel his presence, his being, his radiant warmth. And his youth. Jesus is younger than me, in my contemplation, thin, frail, fresh, my friend, but also my brother. I see myself as servant, brother, and—dare I write this?—friend. This is not something one can talk about publicly, and in light of my horrendous sins, my cold treatment of those I love, it remains an unfathomable mystery. And yet, it is true. I am his friend. So was Merton. So was Dorothy Day. So were Romero and Jean Donovan and Ita Ford. So are Dan Berrigan and countless other Christians, including my parents and friends and Jesuit brothers and Catholic Workers and Plowshares activists and all the poor of the world. We are his community. It is a communion of love. I see him smiling as I write this. . . .

The sky has grown overcast again. The sun is disappearing. The fire has gone out, and it is cold again. I shall have some juice and fruitcake to celebrate this November morning.

Later. The fire burns in the heater, and I've lit a candle beside me on the desk. The flame is reflected several times in the window, so when I look out, I see the trees and the hills through the flames. They are on fire. Every bush is burning. Nature itself experiences the flames of Pentecost. I sip my apple juice in wonder.

Christ, you are smiling. You perceive me through eyes filled with love. Your hands and feet, wounded and scarred, are gentle. Your face looks both angelic and real—human. You are young, youthful. Your voice is truth. You are humble, meek, and radiant in your silence, your purity. You are glorious. You are simple and quiet, modest and shy. You come to me vulnerable, solicitous, not anxious or in a rush, perfectly present.

I long to serve you, to be your friend, to receive you, to welcome you, to be with you through eternity. I want to share you with everyone, with the whole human race. Most of all, I want to please you. I hope that you will take me to yourself and do with me what you will, that you will keep me ever by your side, as your servant, your companion, your faithful friend, and intimate confidant. I only want you. I want to come to you. I want to live for you and die for you and into you. I belong to you.

I am yours. Take me forever into your heart. Let me be one with you, for you are my Lord and my Savior, my God and my All.

This house still stands
not like the one in New Mexico—
tried by fire, tested by a blast from hell—
or the houses of Hiroshima—
gone in a flash—
or the houses of Guajila—
bombed or burned,
like El Mozote—I saw them—
by death's grim soldiers.

No, this house stands tall,
keeps watch,
a lookout post,
perfect for voices
crying in the wilderness:
Repent, repent.
Your peace,
your peace,
at long last,
comes.

I think of St. Francis and my pilgrimage last year to Assisi. These hills and prayerful days remind me of the spirit of peace I discovered in Assisi. For eight days, I walked the streets, sat in church corners, strolled through the fields, and meditated each day at Francis' grave. My soul was lifted, my spirit exalted in the Lord, in peace. I breathed Francis' peace prayer.

Though I was attending a peace conference (to mark the fiftieth anniversary of Pax Christi International), I spent the days quietly to myself, not attending meetings, but meditating on Francis' life, visiting the shrines, learning something about Pax Christi. I explored every nook and cranny, from San Damiano, to the Basilica of St. Clare, to the caves of the distant hills, where Francis and his friends lived and prayed. Several mornings I climbed the hill with friends, watched the sun rise, and joined the circle for song and praise. Each afternoon, I drank cappuccino in the plaza and laughed with my friends, Janice and Roni. The whole experience was not unlike these days, including the peace, the example of a committed life (Merton), the spiritual consolation, and the time with friends (here, Brother Patrick and the other monks). Ineffable joy. Serenity!

I remember my first visit to the Portiuncula. Stepping into the small, hand-built, stone chapel, dwarfed within the sanctuary of the Basilica of Our Lady of Angels, I step back in time into the life of Francis, into the Gospel, into grace. Francis built these walls, placing these stones together. He prayed here, enraptured in joy and peace. His chapel became the center of his life and his order, the holy ground for which, legend holds, he acquired a special papal indulgence granting God's unconditional grace to all those who worship here. I am lifted out of myself, into the heavens, into the presence of Christ. Such deep inner peace! A great blessing. I do not have the words to describe it. Hours pass by as I sit in the corner, immune to the tourists who wander in and out. These stones cry out: *Blessed is the one who comes in the name of the Lord!* My head is bowed, my eyes closed. I adore my God and, finally, step outside into the Italian sunshine, eager once more to live the Gospel—in poverty, simplicity, gratitude, and nonviolence; reconciling all, healing all, affirming all, loving all, praising God every minute with joy.

I do not have adequate words to describe Merton's hermitage either or its effect on me. I write feverishly at this table—I have not written a journal so intensely since I was in jail two years ago. I stumble. I feel speechless, inadequate to the task of recording the grace of these days. I let the words flow, granting me peace, helping me to make sense of the mystery and grace of these hours. Perhaps it will help me in desolate days ahead to remember the peace of these hours and to trust more in Christ.

In two weeks, I will meet with my provincial. He may allow me to accept an offer to teach one semester of theology to freshmen at Fordham University, starting in January, before moving next summer to Northern Ireland for my tertianship year. I feel detached because of the inner peace

I am experiencing. I know that Christ guides me and calls me and that I can remain a contemplative and go deeper into his spirit wherever I am, whatever mission calls me. The main thing is to seek Christ, to stay with Christ, to let Christ work through me, to surrender myself over and over again to Christ. Jesus is all that matters, for I have been to the mountaintop.

Today is the last day of hunting season. Four shots just rang out. Make that five.

I open John Howard Griffin's biography, *Follow the Ecstasy: Thomas Merton, The Hermitage Years, 1965–1968*, to this passage, written during Merton's first week here as a full-time hermit:

> My first obligation is to be myself and follow God's grace and not allow myself to become the captive of some idiot idea, whether of the hermit life or anything else. What matters is not spirituality, not religion, not perfection, not success or failure at this or that, but simply God, and freedom in God's Spirit. (p. 48)

Griffin sums up Merton's solitude, and then quotes Merton's journal, from his first week as a hermit:

> The greatest joy of the solitary life did not come from the quiet, the peace it produced in one's heart, but in awakening and attuning the heart to the voice of God, "to the inexplicable, quite definite inner certitude of one's call to obey God, to hear God, to worship God here, in silence and alone, and that this is the whole reason for one's existence. This makes one's existence fruitful and gives fruitfulness to all one's other acts, and is the

ransom and purification of one's heart that has been dead in sin." (p. 36).

With faith, living in solitude becomes an eschatological gift. I have never before really seen what it means to live in the new creation and in the kingdom. Impossible to explain. If I tried, I would be unfaithful to the grace of it for I would be setting limits to it. It is limitless, without determination, without definition. It is what you make of it each day in response to the Holy Spirit. (p. 42)

I look out the window. It is impossible to explain. Before me lies a sign of the new creation, the promised land—a vision of the reign of peace and love, the possibility of sight, freedom from blindness. None of these words explain or approach my meaning. This place is beyond words, beyond silence, the purity of peace itself. It is a gift, eschatological, but here and now, too. And it summons me to proclaim its wisdom, the gift of peace to the whole human family.

On August 25, 1965, the first day of his new hermit life, Merton concluded his last conference to the novices with these closing words:

> When you pray for me, all I ask that you pray for is that above all I should completely forget my own will and completely surrender to the will of God, because . . . this is all I want to do. I don't want to go up there and just sit and learn a new form of prayer or something like that. It is a question of total surrender to God. I in my turn will pray for you to do the same thing. . . . The ambition of those Greek monks on Mt. Athos is that you get to the

point where you are kissed by God. That is our goal too. (pp. 45–46)

I know what he means. In his hermitage, God bends down from the heavens and kisses me, embraces my soul, holds me in his hand, and then, in Christ, looks on me and smiles. I attribute this in large measure to the prayers of the monks, the prayers of my own Jesuit friends, my parents, and the two or three other friends who know that I'm here. Also, Merton's own prayers. I pray at his grave each morning after Mass and trust that he intercedes for me. God blesses me.

May all the world be so blessed. May all my friends and family be so blessed. May all the poor, the sick, the lonely, the imprisoned, the hungry, the homeless, the refugees, the persecuted, the tortured, the marginalized be so blessed. May all who seek God, may all who live be so blessed, "full measure, pressed down, shaken together and running over."

Merton moved into the woods, Griffin suggests, "not to find God in the silence and solitude, but because he believed that is where God wanted to find him" (p. 46).

The fields are filled with different kinds of birds. I recognize the cardinals and blue jays, but not the large brown birds with white tails. They all turn to look at me when I open the door and step out. For a split second, we study each other, then they all fly off. Now, after fixing the fire, I hear one of them making a racket walking around the roof.

Reading the Griffin biography, I read of the pain, despair, and utter devastation which Merton suffered when he suddenly fell head over heels in love with a beautiful young nurse while he was recovering in the hospital after back surgery, how he sweated out the months that followed and lay awake night after night in unbearable loneliness, thinking of her. I read of the pain of the inevitable break, and the grief he suffered the following year.

Instead of being scandalized as some are by Merton's relationship, I am deeply moved and inspired by Merton's courage to fall freely in love, to celebrate it, to allow himself to be shattered completely for the first time in his life, and to search for God in these deep waters. Brother Patrick spoke of this the other day. Merton survived this traumatic gift and was faithful until the end. He lived it all, suffered greatly, but became more human because of it.

The year was 1966. In the next few years, thousands of men left the priesthood to get married, including two of my uncles. Merton was living out the reality of the crisis in the North American church. He rode it through with grace and charity toward the young woman and himself, and he saw the whole episode as integral to the truth of his life journey to God. She taught him that he was lovable and that he could give love. She showed him how to love. He gave thanks for that essential lesson, as painful as it was. Today, in his house, I feel compassion for him—in his loneliness, obedience, and suffering—and for her, too. I do not view Merton in the inhuman aura of hagiography, in some kind of cult mentality, but rather as a brother on the journey who plumbed the depths of his soul and shares his love and faith with the whole human family. He went ahead of me and all of us, and I can see more clearly and stand taller thanks to his faithful journey.

St. Luke writes that in pain, as he dies on the cross, Jesus consoles the poor man with him. "Amen, I say to you, today you will be with me in paradise"(23:43). Then, in agony, but in a spirit of faithful love and steadfast nonviolence—even joy, Gandhi would say—Jesus cries out, "Father, into your hands I commend my spirit"(23:46). How beautiful! How noble a death! Jesus centers himself in God, humbly trusts in God, and hands himself over peacefully to God. Imagine God receiving the Spirit of Jesus! Here at last, the truest human spirit, a reflection of God's own self, a real son.

I think, too, of Henri Nouwen's bold insight in his book, *The Return of the Prodigal Son*, where he describes Jesus himself as the prodigal son who left his heavenly father, went into the world, and returned home, poor, broken, alone, destitute, repentant. Imagine God, seeing Jesus from afar, running out to greet him, throwing the royal cloak around him, putting a ring on his finger, kissing him, embracing him, offering a feast for him, a banquet in his honor that lasts forever.

Yes, this is what happened. It is the reality of Christ, the Human One. I want to join that heavenly banquet and celebrate Christ's faithful love, his truth-telling, nonviolent resistance to evil, his forgiveness, compassion, and glorious resurrection.

I sit upright in the rocking chair for an hour (1:45–2:45 P.M.), centered, at peace, listening to Christ's words from the cross, praying, "Remember me when you come into your kingdom." He smiles. He sends his loving spirit, his peace, his compassion upon me. This is heaven—an inner glimpse of heaven on earth, the reign of God, here and now, come at last, in a flash of lightning.

The beauty of the solitary life, trees that say nothing and skies that are neutral, is that you can throw away all the masks and forget them until you return among people.

—Thomas Merton, June 1966

I take a long walk across the field to the monastery and out into the woods. On the way, I turn and look back at the hermitage and feel consolation and joy. I taste the peace of resurrection. After praying at Merton's grave and drinking a cup of hot chocolate in the guest house, I walk up to St. Joseph's hill, then across the road, through the old farm and stables and into the woods. In 1989, there were cows and horses everywhere. They are gone now, and the stables have been abandoned.

I pass St. Bernard's field, go over the hill and into the woods, near St. Edmond's field. I hear gun shots. Yikes! I experience the Zen effect of being fair game on this last day of hunting season. My eyes pop open as my head shakes quickly side to side. I am afraid, but I laugh, too, at the thought of dying while on retreat. I walk through the woods, now on a main path, and stop and pray at the statue of Our Lady of Lourdes, next to the stone engraved with the greeting, "Pax." I walk on, along the edge of Monk's Pond, across the road and up the path and hill back to the hermitage. The sun is shining and descending; it is a magnificent fall afternoon, nearly 5 P.M. In the distance, I hear dogs barking on the hunt and an occasional gun shot. Even worse, all afternoon—and now as I write these words—I hear the loud thuds of artillery practice in the distance at Fort Knox or some other military base. Merton complained about this in his journals, and I sympathize. Sometimes, the ground shakes. The world and all its violence are not far away. They surround me here at the house of peace, convincing me to walk farther on along the journey of active yet contemplative nonviolence.

The sun shines through the dead trees over the hill to my right, as I sit on the front porch. The blue sky overhead and the layers of white clouds paint a beautiful picture of peace.

Through the trees to the south of the house, the sky turns pink, then purple. Straight up, over the field in front, the moon shines. I enjoy a delicious dinner: cream of mushroom soup with onion and pepper mixed in, Trappist cheese and crackers, a piece of fruitcake, a tangerine, and pineapple juice. A fire in the heater warms the room. The candle burns brightly. I am cut off from the world and can scarcely believe that one week ago I walked the streets of Manhattan, lost in the crowds, alone in my despair. Here, alone in the peace of these woods, with the sunset and the sky and the moon, I feel hopeful, rested, reassured, certainly not lonely, but comforted and consoled. The sky looks more beautiful each time I glance out the window.

What is the sound of listening? A resonating silence, like the infinite fine line between a grey sky and the ocean, where the horizon cannot be distinguished. My soul blends into the silence around me. Into that silence comes a voice: "I love you. Do not be afraid. I am with you. I give you my peace. You are always with me." The words sound sweet and tender, gentler than any human voice.

I sit in Merton's rocking chair in the center of his room, my reflection and the candlelight looking back at me in the windows. I breathe. I close my eyes. I am completely still. I see in my mind's eye a pair of hands which I hold gently in my own hands. They are wounded. Gentle hands, badly scarred, deeply hurt. For the longest time, this intimacy lingers. The voice speaks: "See. Believe. Doubt no longer. Look at my hands. I live on. I am here. Be at peace." I study the hands.

My mind turns to other hands. I remember visiting with Mother Teresa in Rome last year. I had not seen her for years, yet we have talked on the phone and corresponded regularly about the death penalty, preparing her repeated interventions with government officials on behalf of the condemned. She is badly stooped and frail. That May morning in Rome, a friend introduces me to her while a crowd of a hundred priests and nuns from her order stand around us. She reaches up and puts her hands on my face, one on each cheek, and holds them there while she smiles broadly and gazes into my face, for what seems like a long time.

"Fr. John," she says. "What did we say to the governors?" she asks with a beaming smile.

"'Do what Jesus would do,'" I reply.

"And what happened?"

"Several were granted stays; one was granted clemency."

She looks into my eyes. I have rarely felt such unconditional love. Just last month, she wrote me regarding Sr. Sylvia who died in a car crash in Virginia. Now, Mother is sick and I keep her in my prayers.

In recent years, only two others have held my face in their hands, a long-time activist woman friend and my grandmother, the second to last time I saw her, when she was dying. I noticed their hands. I felt their love. I rarely experience such tenderness.

The hands of the Lord. They reach up and touch my face. Gently, lovingly. "My Lord and my God," I whisper. I feel like the formerly blind man of John's Gospel. Touched and healed, he looks into the eyes of the Lord and falls to the ground in worship.

The silence continues. The fire burns quietly. I see two or three flickering lights in the distant hills, miles away. I am alone, with no TV, no phone, no newspaper, no magazines, no radio, no videos, no films, no music, no mail, no contact with anyone.

"Blessed are you. Blessed are you. Blessed," says the silence.

Ascension Thursday, 1967. One year after his relationship with his nurse friend is resolved, Merton is back writing in his journal: "Peace, silence, freedom of heart, no care, quiet joy." I know precisely these feelings all day today, staying here in the hermitage, walking in the field, standing in the yard, wandering in the woods around the house, sitting on the porch, fidgeting with the fire. I have experienced such peace only rarely in the last fifteen years of my life. I get caught up in the world, overly anxious, deeply insecure, worried about the slightest matter. Such anxiety left my nerves shot at the end of each day at the Sacred Heart Center. The fundraising needs, the maintenance and personnel crises, and the endless pressures crushed my spirit.

I was not nervous, however, last month at the benefit rock concert for the Sacred Heart Center featuring my friend, the singer-songwriter Jackson Browne and popular pianist Bruce Hornsby. Jackson is shy and quiet, the eye in the storm. As the date approached and a million tasks needed to be done, I tried to maintain that same mindful peace. I was somewhat successful. Meanwhile, not only did we raise a tremendous amount of money for the neighborhood poor and sell out the thirty-six hundred-seat Landmark Theater auditorium, the musicians were in top form, excited to be playing for one another. The show began at eight and did not finish until after midnight. Their music was beautiful, from the jazz piano runs of Bruce Hornsby to the haunting lyrics of Jackson, as in "Too Many Angels," "Late for the Sky," and "For a Dancer." Jackson was all heart—generous, kind, thoughtful, and glad to be of service. The evening was a high note for all of us and an upbeat conclusion to my time in Richmond.

But for someone concerned about peace, alas, I rarely radiate it. In this paradise, however, I experience peace of heart. Yet I am not a Trappist. My Jesuit vocation thrusts me into the hurricane of the world. I must struggle to live this inner peace of heart when I return to world's hurricane of injustice. I must discipline myself to cling to inner peace. I need to take time away, to schedule annual retreats farther in advance, and to protect my solitude. I know it is possible. I must work harder to set the conditions of such peace.

There is in all visible things an invisible fecundity, a dimmed light, a meek namelessness, a hidden wholeness. This mysterious Unity and Integrity is Wisdom, the Mother of all, Natura naturans. There is in all things an inexhaustible sweetness and purity, a silence that is a fountain of action and of joy. It rises up in wordless gentleness and flows out to me from the unseen roots of all created being.
—Thomas Merton

Thursday

At 4:30 A.M. it is dark, quiet, and cold. The fire has long since died. I go to the monastery in awe and wonder, giving thanks for this new day, born in peace.

8 A.M. I walk back from the monastery to the hermitage in the pouring rain, completely soaked, but happy and content. I am grateful to be here, to celebrate Eucharist, to visit with my friend, Patrick, over coffee. I am grateful for the blessing of rain, the green earth, the Spirit of life exuding from creation. A dark wet morning, but beautiful.

At Laudes, we read Psalm 100. It could be the song of all the monks living at Gethsemani. Certainly, it is the song of Merton living here in this house, writing essays on peace, denouncing war and racism, pursuing the nonviolent alternative with the force of silence itself. The satyagraha of Merton! I want it to be my psalm, too:

My song is of mercy and justice;
I sing to you, O God.
I will walk in the way of compassion.
When, O God, will you come?

I will walk with blameless heart
within my house;
I will not see before my eyes
whatever is base.

I will hate the ways of the crooked;
they shall not be my friends.
The false-hearted must keep far away;
the wicked I disown.

The one who slanders his neighbor in secret
I will bring to silence.
The one of proud looks and haughty heart
I will never endure.

I look to the faithful in the land
that they may dwell with me.
The one who walks in the way of compassion
shall be my friend.

No one who practices deceit
shall live within my house.
No one who utters lies shall stand
before my eyes.
Morning by morning I will silence
all the wicked in the land,
uprooting from the city of God
all who do evil.

What is the sound of listening? It is the gentle, steady, per-
sistent rain, falling quietly on the roof. It is creation listening

to the voice of God. It is the sound of peace. I hear it tapping the roof, falling outside, blessing upon blessing, mercy upon mercy, grace upon grace.

Prayer is like the rain. It just happens, peacefully, a gift given and received quietly. It washes the soul clean and places it in the glow of peace. All is made sparkling new. The spirit shines, soothed and comforted.

God is like the rain—all-embracing, pure gift, quiet, life-giving, coming from above, greater than us, but much gentler, as on a morning like this.

Also at Laudes, a monk read from Proverbs, chapter 9:

Wisdom has built herself a house.
She has erected her seven pillars.
She has slaughtered her beasts, prepared her wine.
She has laid her table.
She has dispatched her maidservants
and proclaimed from the city's height:
"Who is ignorant? Let him step this way."
To the fool, she says,
"Come and eat my bread,
drink the wine I have prepared!
Leave your folly and you will live,
walk in the ways of perception. . . .
The fear of Yahweh is the beginning of wisdom;
the knowledge of the Holy One—perception indeed!"
(Prv 9:1–6, 10)

I turn to the book of Wisdom to the meditate on Hagia Sophia:

Wisdom is bright, and does not grow dim.
By those who love her, she is readily seen,
and by those who look for her.

Quick to anticipate those who desire her, she makes herself
    known to them.
Watch for her early and you will have no trouble;
you will find her sitting at your gates;
even to think about her is understanding fully grown;
be on the alert for her and anxiety will quickly leave you.
She herself walks about looking for those who are worthy of her
and graciously shows herself to them as they go,
in every thought of theirs coming to meet them. . . .
She is an inexhaustible treasure
and those who acquire wisdom win God's friendship,
commended as they are to God by the benefits of her
    teaching. . . .
All that is hidden, all that is plain, I have come to know,
instructed by wisdom who designed them all.
For within her is a spirit intelligent, holy, unique, manifold,
    subtle,
active, incisive, unsullied, lucid, invulnerable, beneficent,
    loving to people,
steadfast, dependable, unperturbed, almighty, all-surveying,
penetrating all intelligent, pure and most subtle;
for wisdom is quicker to move than any motion;
She is so pure, she pervades and permeates all things.
She is a breath of the power of God,
pure emanation of the glory of the Almighty. . . .
She is a reflection of the eternal light,
untarnished mirror of God's active power,
image of God's goodness. . . .
In each generation she passes into holy souls,
she makes them friends of God and prophets;
for God loves the one who lives with wisdom. (Wis 6–7)

In the guesthouse library, I come upon a quote from St.
Gregory Nazianan: "The will of God is our peace." Amen.

For the feast, the Memorial of the Presentation of Mary, Luke's Gospel was read. Jesus' mother and brothers come to see him. He looks at his disciples and says, "Who are my mother and brothers? Whoever does the will of God is brother and sister and mother to me." My prayer this morning is that I may do the will of God, that I may live with wisdom, that I may always know God's peace, and so, become one day a friend of God, a brother of Jesus.

After coffee and a slice of nut bread with Brother Patrick, I linger in the retreatants' dining room, where Merton's voice speaks over the sound system. "The basic thing is an awakened heart," he explains, (probably sometime in 1964). "Instead of constantly thinking of God as a concept, cultivate an awareness of love. That is continuous prayer. . . . Once you have found a way to do it quietly, peacefully, keep on doing it for the rest of your life. . . . This is the pearl of great price, the love of God. Don't worry about knowledge of God, as the Sufis say. Rather seek personal experience of God in an awareness of love."

I feel like a novice listening to Merton. I have miles to go on my journey toward an awakened heart, an awareness of love. The gift of these days encourages me to carry on with faith and confidence.

What have I learned here? I am learning the wisdom of the ages, relearning lessons as old as these hills. My teachers are the rain, this house, the green valley, the monks, the psalms, the Gospel, the spirit of peace, and Hagia Sophia herself.

First, I experience the beauty of silence. In silence, I find peace. I learn to listen. I wait for the voice of God. My wounds are healed. I become again my true self. I see myself as I am—a sinner, yes, but beloved by God as a son and a friend. In silence, I taste the banquet of heaven. I learn to breathe again, and breathing becomes significant. The world falls away, with all its noise and idolatry. Nature reveals herself because I am reduced to nothing. Then in that stillness, I hear creation praising God, and slowly, gently, without even knowing it, I join in. Life becomes a marvelous celebration, a great dance, a festival of peace. All worries, all fears, all anxieties, all violence fade away, and I enter the solitude of God. What a beautiful gift. We are all created for this peace. We are summoned to enter the house of God where the great celebration is taking place. The path to this feast is uphill and taken in silence.

Second, I learn that solitude leads to inner freedom. Here alone in these woods, away from the maddening crowd, the roar of the imperial lions, nestled by the fire in this hermitage, I discover who I am. I am myself. I live. I breathe. I eat. I sleep. I pray. I sit, and I am not lonely because I realize with a new contemplative awareness that I am in the presence of God. I am doing nothing. For once, I stop doing things. There is an exhilarating freedom in such simplicity. I catch a glimpse of God, and I realize that, ah! God has been here all along. My distractions, my busyness, my rat-race inner life have prevented me from pursuing this inner realization. Solitude sets the stage for God's coming, God's breaking into our hearts. Solitude makes possible the inner transformation I seek. Solitude takes us to greater communion with God.

Third, I learn to be present. I am not usually fully present to those around me. Instead, I get absorbed with the cares of the world, a busy schedule, phone calls, letters, meetings, lectures to give, trips to take, and books to be read. I rush about, thinking of the past, worrying about the future, rarely attuned to the present. How absurd! There is no past, no future, no sense of time. Life is lived in the present moment. Here I remember, Of Course! that life is be lived like this all the time. I must retreat into silence and solitude to relearn these basics. Jesus requires that I be in the world, but not of it: fully present, calm, centered, attentive to those around me, living life to the full, breathing in and out, a contemplative, aware at all times.

Fourth, I experience peace of heart. It is a gift freely given. For all my efforts, I cannot attain it on my own. I am proud, deceitful, violent, and judgmental. But here in the hermitage, in the setting of the valley and the monastic prayers, as I break down and confess my faults and accept my weaknesses, there she is: Peace. I hope and pray that I can mature through suffering and love, prayer and silence, so that this peace, this gift of the risen Christ, will rest permanently in my heart. This is my great desire: that I always reflect and radiate the peace of Christ. From this peace of heart, I can go forward into the world and share peace, build peace, make peace, be peace.

Fifth, I feel a need for love, "the great commandment." Now I remember—God loves me. I am God's beloved. We are all the beloved children of God. Our response? We are invited to love God with all our hearts, our minds, our souls, and our strength. I realize how poorly I show love for God, but the Spirit of Christ within me loves God through me. This hermitage prepares me to be a better lover of God. And I want to go deeper into that love for God and taste God's unconditional love for me and the whole human family, so that one day I may be lost in that Love for eternity.

That great call extends to love for all others. In this solitude, I see myself as I am. I know my sins. I understand that I have hurt people, especially those close to me, and that I continue to hurt them. This silence encourages me not to give up, but to try again to love others, quietly, humbly, with my whole heart, to love my family and friends and community members, my neighbors and all I meet, the poor and the marginalized, and most of all, my enemies; to let myself burn with a gentle love for all.

Sixth, I find that compassion is everything. At this Polonnaruwa, the Spirit shows compassion to me, and I feel freer to become more compassionate toward others. I see again how often I fail at compassion, how rarely I feel the pain of others, enter into their lives with a loving presence, and give generously to others without any regard for myself. Here, for a moment, I am lifted beyond myself, my agenda, my anger, my condemnation of others, my lack of love— and shown a better way, a new possibility, the way of compassion. I have known this intellectually for years. But I have barely begun to put it into practice. It is still the hardest task in life and, yet, the most noble. This is my prayer, the hope instilled in me through the silence of this cottage: to live a life of real compassion for all people. I believe it must be possible to attain such compassion, otherwise God would not stir up such desire within me and others. And so, once again, I vow to walk the way of compassion.

Seventh, I know the possibilities of nonviolence. I never stop marveling at its simplicity, its potential, its ultimate truth. I hear it from Gandhi, Dr. King, and Dorothy Day. I experience it here in Merton's house. I pray for a new spirit of nonviolence to be born in the hearts of the next generation, in the churches, in our country. I come here thinking of the carnage in Rwanda, the suffering refugees in Zaire, the hatred in Northern Ireland,

Palestine, and Bosnia, the injustices in East Timor and Sri Lanka; the poverty of Africa, Latin America, and Asia; the racism and sexism in our own country; and most of all, our militarism, our ongoing government expenditure of billions upon billions of dollars for weapons of mass destruction while millions of people are starving and homeless and miserable. I want to live nonviolently and, like Merton, to be a witness for nonviolence, an apostle of nonviolence, to call others to repent of our terrible violence, to disarm and learn the way of peace.

Eighth, I hear again the call to humility. I am summoned to let go of my pride, my self-righteousness, my egotism, my self-serving ambition. Alone in these woods, I feel powerless and helpless, and this is a blessing. It is only in the last year or so, lost in the all-consuming work of the Sacred Heart Center, that I have caught a glimpse of my great blind-spot: an appalling pride and egotism. There I was too busy to parade around in an air of self-righteousness. I am probably the most self-righteous person I know, yet I have been under the illusion these last twenty years that I am holy and humble. The reality is exactly the opposite, as my family, friends, and some fellow Jesuits know. I walk around with a chip on my shoulder thinking, sometimes saying, "How come the rest of you aren't living the Gospel as well as I am? Why don't you do as I do?" I am ashamed of myself. The invitation to humility which comes with solitude, silence, and peace is liberating. A lifeline, it comes with the hope of salvation.

Finally, I have unbounded hope. For the first time in ages, I feel hopeful—not just for my immediate future, but for my life, the lives of my family and friends, the lives of all who live and breathe. I attribute this hope, given to me in the silence and solitude of Merton's hermitage, to one thing: the Resurrection. The Lord has not been destroyed forever. Yes, he was killed, but now He lives. I know this in my heart.

The silence, the peace, the solitude, the rain, the hermitage, the valley, the hills, the stars, and the sun testify to Christ's resurrection. Merton, too, lives on, as do all disciples, all people of faith, hope, and love, all people of compassion and peace. Today, I realize this truth. One day, after I'm dead and gone from this world, I, too, along with the whole human race, shall join that new life. I shall dance and sing at the eternal feast of the Lord's resurrection. Like everyone, I, too, will share in his resurrection. As I share his cross, as I walk the way of nonviolence and compassion, seek justice and peace, resist evil, speak the truth, and disarm the idols, as I enter the Paschal Mystery in discipleship to my Lord, I know resurrection awaits me and the whole human race. This morning, I am filled with hope. Come what may, all will be well.

I pick up Merton's small copy of *Thoreau* (a hardcover 1947 portable edition of collected works). It is old, broken, worn. I read the introduction. "Walking in the woods, and alone —living as a poet—was his business." On the margin, a faded "X" has been penciled in next to this sentence. His book, *A Natural History of Massachusetts,* is likewise marked. Sentences describing nature, birds, the woods, and life in the spirit are also noted, such as this: "Surely joy is the condition of life." "In winter we lead a more inward life."

Here Merton read *On the Duty of Civil Disobedience,* a book I first discovered in history class as a junior at Duke University and then again in the Jesuit Novitiate, where I was eager to practice its wisdom. Merton marked Thoreau's nature books, *A Winter Walk* (1843); *Life in the Wilderness* (1848); *A Week on the Concord and Merrimack Rivers* (1849): *A Yankee in Canada* (1853); and *Journal* (1858). In *Walden,* a few key passages are underlined: "To be a philosopher is not merely to have subtle thoughts nor even to found a school, but so to love wisdom as to live according to its dictates, a life of simplicity, independence, magnanimity, and trust." And this: "There is some of the same fitness in a person's building his own house that there is in a bird's building its own nest. Who knows but if people constructed their dwellings with their own hands and provided food for themselves and their families simply and honestly enough, the poetic faculty would be universally developed, as birds universally sing when they are so engaged?"

The only dog-eared page contains Thoreau's life summation: "I went to the woods because I wished to live deliberately, to front only the essential facts of life, and see if I could not learn what I had to teach, and not, when I came to die, discover that I had not lived. I did not wish to live what was not life, living is so dear; nor did I wish to practice resignation, unless it was quite necessary. I wanted to live deeply and suck out all the marrow of life, to live so sturdily and Spartan like as to put to rout all that was not life."

Noon. The rain appears to have stopped. I discover some popping corn in the cabinet and make popcorn. However, I misjudge the amount of corns to put in the pot, and it overflows. It fills a second pot.

In silence, from 10:30–11:30, I meditate on the resurrection of Jesus from John 21. The scene is not unlike my view—idyllic, contemplative, Buddhist. "On the shore stood Jesus, and it was morning." Imagine. He has just been arrested, jailed, tried, tortured, and executed. His community of friends betrayed him, denied him, and fled in his hour of need. Yet here he is now, standing by the shore at the Sea of Galilee, at dawn. He tells them, as they struggle to fish, where to cast their nets. After a long fruitless night, they suddenly catch a boat-load. They recognize him. "When they climbed out on shore," we are told, "they saw a charcoal fire with fish on it and bread." "Bring some of the fish you just caught," he tells them. Then, this: "Come, have breakfast." "Jesus came over, and took the bread and gave it to them, and in like manner, the fish."

What a beautiful scene! The peace and gentle quiet of it. What strikes me today is what is not said. There is no word of reprimand, revenge, anger, judgment, condemnation, no sign of hurt or guilt, but something entirely different: Breakfast! Jesus quietly serves a morning meal to the friends who had abandoned him. They were silent, we are told, and asked him nothing.

I remember camping along the Sea of Galilee in the summer of 1982, during Israel's war with Lebanon. At dawn each morning for a week, I swam in the cool, blue lake waters. The sun rose as an orange ball over the sea. Those days were filled with contemplative grace, like my days of solitude here or on Block Island. This scene is filled with a quiet, profound grace. What is important is what is not said and the action: our Lord serves a meal. He has just risen from the dead—the most dramatic act in the history of the world—and quietly, mindfully, peacefully, he builds a fire, cooks some fish, and invites them to breakfast. What a God we have! So caring, so compassionate, so *human*. The joy and tranquility of the scene. A new day indeed!

But it does not end there. To Peter, who has denied knowing him three times, he asks three times the great question: Do you love me? Do you love me? Do you truly love me? Jesus uses the Greek word for love, *agape*, that unconditional, sacrificial, active love for all humanity. Peter responds with the Greek word for love, *philia*, the love between friends: protective, guarded, limited. Finally, he says to Peter: "Feed my lambs, feed my sheep." and "When you were young, you dressed yourself and went where you wanted, but when you grow old, you will stretch out your hands and someone else will put a belt around you and take you where you would rather not go. . . . Follow me" (Jn 21:1–19).

As I ponder the text and write out these words, I hear the thick Dutch accent of Henri Nouwen, leading us in a long morning meditation at the May, 1985 Sojourners Peace Pentecost gathering in Washington, D.C. Every year or so, I have replayed a tape of that talk. He spoke enthusiastically about Jesus' question to Peter. It touched me deeply because the next day I flew for the first time to El Salvador, where I spent a week with the University Jesuits (who were later assassinated) and worked for two months in an Archdiocesan refugee camp. Henri kept repeating Christ's question, "Do you love me?" and calling us to hear the urgent cry of God. "This is Christ's most important question, especially for people who care about peace and justice," he exclaimed. "We have to hear the urgency, the longing, the searching in Christ's voice. We need to listen to this question." All summer long, in the heat and terror of the camp, as I worked in the fields with displaced Salvadorans, as bombs fell around us and death squad soldiers periodically questioned us, I heard that question—"Do you love me?"—and its answer—"Someday, someone will put a belt around you and take you were you would rather not go."

On my last day in El Salvador, one of the refugee families presented me with a handmade belt, made out of the material they use to make hammocks. I was deeply moved and immediately remembered Jesus' question (and Henri's passionate talk). Christ, present in the poor of El Salvador, was taking me by the hand and leading me—a first-world, upper-class, well-educated, white, North American, male cleric—where I would rather not go: to the cross, to nonviolent resistance against United States warmaking. Through their pain and joy, Christ spoke to me then as he does today, calling me to discipleship. The invitation is simple: "Follow me."

Six weeks ago, on September 21, Henri Nouwen died. I had hoped to visit him this month. He had just sent me a copy of his latest book, *Can You Drink the Cup?*, and I immediately wrote him a letter with arrangements to visit him in Toronto. He never received my letter. He suffered a massive heart attack in Holland while traveling to Russia to film a documentary about the Rembrandt painting and his book, *The Return of the Prodigal Son.* So I drove from Richmond to Toronto to attend his funeral. With a circle of family, community members, and friends, I shoveled the wet dirt into his grave and prayed the Lord's prayer. He loved God well, went where he would rather not have gone, and became a disciple of Jesus.

This morning, in silence, I hear the question of Christ. "Do you love me?" Yes, Lord Jesus, I love you. I love you. You know everything. You know well that I love you, that I would love you with *agape!* Once again, the mission: feed, tend, follow.

The sublime grace of resurrection: first, a quiet breakfast; then, a vulnerable, intimate exchange; finally, an invitation: "You take up the journey. It's your turn now. You try it. Start from Galilee, from the world of the poor, set your face on Jerusalem, against systemic injustice and warmaking, and keep your heart set on me. Speak the truth, heal the poor, reconcile strangers, make peace, forgive all, resist the imperial powers, take up the cross—and I will be with you."

❖

4:20 P.M. After a nap, I work at the fire, finish the kindling, and nearly use up the indoor pile of logs. A stack of wet logs stands on the porch. I may have to resort to them. I read scripture, Merton, and Gandhi, then head out for a walk. The rain has stopped. The sky is gray. It is a cold November day. I walk alone in the woods, lost to the world, as if I've fallen off the face of the earth. I think: "You are a nobody, John. You have accomplished nothing. You are a powerless human being, fumbling about, merely existing." And the realization deepens: "You need not accomplish anything. You can simply be and love all you meet and offer compassion, and that is enough." I look at the pines, the dead trees in the distant hills, the early winter sky. My feet slosh in the puddles. I feel my nothingness. Like the pine trees, I accomplish nothing (as far as the world is concerned). I stand in the world and breathe and count myself lucky, fortunate, blessed.

I think solemnly of Jesus dying on the cross. The bystanders voice their despair and doubt, putting words of challenge to all those who seek nonviolent transformation: "What have you accomplished? If you are the Son of God, then do something. Come down from that cross! Prove it; then we will believe you." They could not be colder, more cruel, more dismissive. This sophisticated, theologically-correct, passive, know-it-all-crowd laughs in disgust: "Puh-leeze! Who does he think he is?" They show no compassion, do not care about the suffering before them, and mock the one who seeks nonviolent social change. They dismiss any possibility of hope and reveal not only their lack of faith in God, but also their lack of love.

Merton suggests a Zen approach, a take-it-or-leave-it attitude, complete detachment from results. The truth, the love, the Spirit of nonviolence, the prayer, the real hope in Christ—these are the things that matter. Stay faithful to the

Way, to the struggle, to a life of nonviolence, and let God do with us whatever God wills.

As I write sitting on the front porch, rain drips down from the roof and lands on the leaves, in regular splats, like a metronome keeping track of creation and my breath. Birds chirp nearby. I intend to keep listening.

I sit here for an over an hour on Merton's wooden chair beneath the "Shalom" sign, next to the front door on the porch, doing nothing. My eyes are wide open. I breathe gently. I'm perched on my chair as if watching a great film, a thriller, on the edge of my seat. I look out at creation. I study dead tree limbs, the birch cross, the aged wagon wheel, the wet leaves, the logs, the three wooden beams that support the roof, the horizon. Such purity, such peace. I grieve for my inability to maintain this peace in my day-to-day life.

A voice whispers to my heart: "I love you, John. I love you so much." It is the Lord! I rejoice and dwell in God's love.

This afternoon, I pray that somehow today and in the remaining few days I might go deeper into God, into the Spirit of Life, the Spirit of peace, the Spirit of Christ. Sitting here, it happens naturally. There is no schedule, no sense of duty, no obligation, no sense of control. It just happens.

What happens? Nothing happens. It is a marvelous, enriching experience, "life-enhancing" as May Sarton would say. I am hidden in creation, tucked away in the woods, watched over the by the angels, blessed by the Holy Spirit's peace, and periodically gifted with a word or two from God. Thank you, God, for these blessings. As Merton said, the whole human race seeks such contemplative peace, but doesn't know it.

A breeze is coming. I can hear it rustle the treetops on Mt. Olivet to my right. It builds up in a kind of rush like the sound of the ocean. There now, as quickly as it blew in, it dies down. It is gone. Beautiful.

I stand and give the ancient native American blessing to the four winds. First, I bless the valley, making the sign of the cross, saying, "Bless you, Creation, in the name of the God of life, the Christ of life, the Holy Spirit of life." Then, to the woods to my right, on top of Mt. Olivet: "Bless you, Creation, in the name of the God of peace, the Christ of peace, the Holy Spirit of peace." Then behind me, to the house: "Bless you, house, in the name of the God of love, the Christ of love, the Holy Spirit of love." Finally, to the woods to the north on my left: "Bless you, Creation, in the name of the God of hope, the Christ of hope, the Holy Spirit of hope."

The bells toll. Vespers begin. The blessings continue.

Night has fallen. The fire roars away. Dinner is served: cream of mushroom soup with onion and spices, with an orange and a tangerine for dessert.

"The great thing in prayer is not to pray but to go directly to God," Merton told the sisters at the Our Lady of the Redwoods monastery in California, just before flying to Asia (as recorded in "Man of Prayer," by David Steindl-Rast, *Thomas Merton: Monk*, ed. Patrick Hart [Kalamazoo, Mich: Cistercian, 1983], 84–89).

> If saying your prayers is an obstacle to prayer, cut it out. Let Jesus pray. Thank God that Jesus is praying. Forget yourself. Enter into the prayer of Jesus. . . . Let prayer pray within you, whether you know it or not. This means a deep awareness of our true inner identity. It implies a life

of faith, but also of doubt. . . . Faith will grow out of doubt, the real doubt. . . . The point is that we need not justify ourselves. By grace we are Christ. Our relationship with God is that of Christ to the Father in the Holy Spirit.

"A Christian is no longer under judgment," Merton concluded. "He need not justify himself. I must remember that I am not condemned, yet that I am worthy of condemnation. How can I live the message of Christian newness in these final days? I am not called to gather merit, but to go all over the world taking away people's debts. We need a theology of liberation, instead of an official debt machine. I belong entirely to Christ. There is no self to justify."

For me, being in this house of prayer, this house of peace, is an act of resistance to the culture of death. The culture is absurd: the world and its mad rush to violence, its greed, its all-consuming consumerism, its inhumanity, its coldness, its nuclear weapons and Trident submarines and Air Force jet bombers and cruise missiles and silos and electric chairs. The world is in love with death. All of us are caught in its hypnotic spell, going about our business, telling ourselves how reasonable the death culture is, how secure we feel in the shadow of the Pentagon, our nuclear arsenal, Wall Street, the SAC base, and our Trident fleet. We have grown used to war and its fallout: executions, starvation, homelessness, prisons, guns, drugs, domestic violence, racism, sexism, homophobia, abortion, torture, and fear of every one. Death is normal; those who resist death and live life are abnormal.

But here, I meet the God of life who calls us to a culture of life, a culture of nonviolence, who calls us to live, first of all, and to let others live in peace with justice. By "fleeing to the hills" as Jesus' recommended, I turn my back on death and its invidious despair. I want something more. I seek God's reign of nonviolence, love and peace, and even more than that, the living God herself. I want union with the God of peace for myself and all living things. I want it to begin here and now, so I must begin with myself and walk up the mountain of God, where God will instruct me in God's ways. As Isaiah explains, after we all come down from our mountaintop encounter with God, the people of God will disarm their weapons, beat their swords into plowshares, and walk in the light of God along the way of nonviolence.

May it one day happen. I pray that I may be a part of the wider faith community which listens to the God of peace on God's holy mountain and then engages in the work of disarmament and peace.

8:00 P.M. In the chapel, wrapped in a brown-knit afghan, like Gandhi in his shawl, I sit before the altar where a candle burns and look at the crucifix and the icons. I pray for people by name, beginning with my father, my mother, family and friends; for all those places of pain and poverty; for all communities of faith and nonviolence; for all resisters of war and injustice; and for the poor of the earth. In silence, at this altar, the Lord hears my plea.

Friday

I walk into the cold darkness around 5 A.M. Halfway down the path, I turn and look back at the hermitage. There stands a house of prayer, a house of peace, the Lord's house. At Laudes, the psalm calls us to rejoice. I vest with the priests and process out to concelebrate morning Mass. I bow at the altar, kiss the altar, take my place near the presider, an old monk with a thick accent and black glasses. We sit attentively during the readings. In this dark, cold chamber at this solemn ceremony, forty white-robed monks, a handful of retreatants, and myself hear an angel tell John of Patmos to eat a small scroll and then to prophesy to peoples, nations, and kings (Rv 10:8–11). Then, Luke describes Jesus' entrance into the Temple: "He proceeded to drive out those who were selling things, saying to them, 'It is written, "My house shall be called a house of prayer but you have made it a den of thieves"'" (Lk 19:45–48).

We sit in silence. The Word is filled with power and action. We are called to prophesy, to speak truth to the nations, to denounce their injustice, their violence, their wars, their greed, their oppression of the poor. In the Temple, Jesus shows us how to prophesy. We are to take direct nonviolent action for the sake of justice, for God's sake. How often I have pondered this scene, written about it, lectured about it. I have used it as a basis for my acts of nonviolent civil disobedience, most recently my Plowshares action. Jesus risks his life in a peaceful, illegal act of civil disobedience, turning over tables in the Temple. In first century Palestine, the Temple was the center of religious, imperial, and economic control. To be a person of faith, you were required to attend religious services in the Temple each year and that meant purchasing the necessary and expensive paraphernalia (the doves, for example). The poor were the ones who suffered under this religious oppression. In his anger, Jesus turns over the tables of the money changers. "My house shall be called a house of prayer," he cries out. "You have made it a den of thieves."

I look up at the long, white sanctuary, where the monks listen in silence. Here is a house of prayer, a house of silence where God is worshiped day and night in Spirit and in truth. Here, too, at this hermitage, stands a house of prayer, silence, and worship.

I've always been impressed by Jesus' dramatic action in the Temple, even though it is so flagrantly ignored and dismissed by the mainstream churches. According to the synoptics, it is the reason for Jesus' arrest and execution. He was killed for this public disruption, this symbolic direct action. As far as movement people were concerned, his resistance bore no immediate result, except for his arrest and death. Business thrived, the oppression continued. Finally, as Jesus foresaw, the Romans obliterated the whole Temple structure. Jesus saw the long term consequences of their greed, their violence, their false worship, and their allegiance to the empire. He pleaded for nonviolence, resistance, true faith in God, honest worship. But they ignored his plea, and the empire annihilated the city. Today he pleas for nuclear disarmament and justice for the poor, warning that this time we are headed for global, environmental destruction. Again, we ignore his warning.

Returning to the hermitage, I let the readings sink in. Yes, I must prophesy to the nations. Yes, I must worship God in God's house of prayer, like this faithful remnant does here. But if Jesus, the One I follow, is so riled up over the injustice of big business in the Temple and the people's compromise with the empire to the point that he offers up his life in an act of civil disobedience—what would he say about our militarism, which continues to destroy God's creation and threatens to destroy the entire planet, and the flipside effect of our insane military arsenal: our oppression of the poor, the forced starvation of more than a billion people around the world? I can only imagine! Jesus must seethe with outrage at the world's violence and injustice.

Prophesy? What else can we do, faced with the global crisis of these times, but call for total military disarmament as well as the disarmament of our hearts and cities? Perhaps this will placate and tame the righteous indignation of the Lord, bring him peace, restore him to his compassionate love for us, and heal his agony. In our prophetic struggle for disarmament, we mediate between humanity and God, running back and forth between the two unreconciled parties, first telling humanity—"Disarm now! Dismantle your weapons, feed the starving, house the homeless, welcome the refugee, liberate the oppressed and the imprisoned, care for the earth, reconcile with everyone, make amends for your wrongdoing, stop the killing, show compassion to all, include everyone in the fabric of society, and walk the way of nonviolence."

And then to God, we plead, "Please forgive us. We are insane. We will work for disarmament and peace as you request. Give us a little more time. You are right. Have mercy on us. We fall on the ground before you and beg you to forgive us. We're sorry. We are blind. Help us to see the way to peace. Disarm our hearts and our world. Help us to be people of nonviolence, so that instead of a world filled with weapons and guns, we can offer you a world of peace as you desire. Come and build among us your house of prayer, your house of peace, where you can dwell among us and feel at home. O God, we beg you, forgive us."

The Prayer of St. Francis: Updated

Lord make me an instrument of your peace—

Let me serve as a channel of your nonviolent love, a reconciler of peoples, an apostle of Gospel nonviolence. Help me to love all people, including my enemies. Use me as a voice and instrument for nuclear and total disarmament. Make me a witness to your way of suffering love and redemptive goodwill. Use me in your struggle to liberate the oppressed, create justice for the poor, resist systemic injustice, topple the idols of death, denounce the gods of war, and beat swords into plowshares. Use me to unmask the false peace of the world, which buries the cry of the poor, the blood of the oppressed, the victims of war. Use me to create your peace, the peace which comes through the nonviolent cross and resurrection. Fashion me into a person of contemplative nonviolence; a person of prayer, mindfulness, harmony, and wisdom. Let me radiate your disarming grace and light and presence to all.

Where there is hatred, let me sow love—

Transform the hatred in my own heart into your love, understanding, compassion, forgiveness, and grace. Disarm me so that hatred disappears and love flows freely to all. Use me to build bridges between divided peoples, to soothe their fears, to see one another as sisters and brothers. Let me sow the seeds of love that will bear fruit in a new spirit of repentance, mercy, disarmament, justice, and liberation for the poor. Extinguish the flames of war and spring forth your life-giving waters of love in the church, between the races and the genders, the rich and the poor, the old and the young, in Baghdad and Washington, D.C., in Calcutta and Mississippi, in Rwanda and East Timor, in Haiti and El Salvador, in South Africa and the Philippines, between East and West, North and South. Help me to sow seeds of agape, compassion, and peace, and to water and care for those seeds that they may flower into your reign of nonviolence.

Where there is injury, let me sow pardon—

That I may forgive seventy times seven times and teach forgiveness by my life; vowing like the Buddha compassion toward all living things for the rest of my life; healing especially those who have lost loved ones to violence and murder, that they may forgive those who murdered their loved ones. May we as a people grant clemency to all, including those who have murdered.

May the death penalty be abolished, deterrence discarded, and the just war theory thrown away. May healing and repentance and forgiveness be the new spirit of the times. May we repent for our use of nuclear weapons on the people of Hiroshima and Nagasaki and apologize; may we pardon all crimes of war and genocide by disarming our arsenal to ensure that they never happen again. May all claim their true identity as your children; and may you continue to forgive us our sins, our rejection of you, and our violence to you on the cross.

Where there is doubt, faith in you—

In the midst of this culture of death—faithless, insecure, fearful, idolatrous, vengeful, arrogant, materialistic; in the doubting church, believing in the culture's empty promises, illusions, material goods, idols of death, the false security of its bombs and militarism instead of you; let me sow seeds of living faith in You. Help us to trust you who remain faithful to us. Let our faith manifest itself in the committed lives we live, true to the Gospel, to your way of nonviolence and suffering love. Let us keep your covenant of peace and remain faithful to you yourself, our gentle father, our loving mother, our faithful God.

Where there is despair, only hope—

Low grade despair and high octane desperation; no win situations with no way out; in the midst of anxiety, panic, loneliness, fear, devastation, poverty, war, death itself— there, let me sow hope, the seeds of resurrection, a way out of no way; new possibilities, new life, the life that overcomes death; the seeds of reconciliation, love, and confident trust in God. Let me instill the gift of peace, the dawn of a new day, the promise of resurrection, the vision of the promised land where there is no more war, no more nuclear weapons, no more violence, no more injustice, no more poverty, no more misery, no more fear—only love and you, the God of resurrection, standing warmly in our midst.

Where there is darkness, light—

Amidst the darkness in our hearts, the sin of violence, our self-hatred, our fear, our hostility toward one another, our oppression of the poor, our rejection of you; let your light shine: the light of peace, joy, love, trust; the light of truth, the light of resurrection, the light of hope. Let us be like Christ, the light of the world, pointing to your presence, showing each other how to live justly, humanly, nonviolently, and compassionately. Let us burn with love, truth, faith, peace, and justice, so that our light, your light, will shine for all, and one day, we will see you face to face.

Where there is sorrow, joy—

In this world of sorrow and grief, desolation and depression, sadness and death, in hearts dulled from hostility and hatred, deadened by the bomb's shadow, by the despair of imperial oppression, the race for money, the loss of love and loved ones; in hearts grown cold by horror upon horror, a nuclear blast upon the human spirit—there, put in us the joy of your resurrection, your joy now complete, the dawn of that new morning, when you stand by the shore, alive, welcoming, forgiving. Let us taste the joy of *shalom* which the world can never take away from us.

O Divine Master—

Jesus; God of Life; Human One; Compassionate, Nonviolent Savior; Prince of Peace; Mercy within Mercy within Mercy; Resister of Evil; the Way, the Truth, and the Life; Good Shepherd; our Beloved, our Brother, our Bread, our Breath.

Grant that I may seek not so much to be consoled as to console—

Not to be the center of attention, to strive for praise and honor, to let my domineering ego, proud and arrogant, run rampant; instead, may I comfort others, bring them peace and warmth, safety and affection, unconditional love and kindness, and not cause anyone to be afraid in my presence, but to be at ease, at peace, relaxed, content because it is not so much me they see, but your presence shining transparently through me. May I speak the truth, denounce injustice, proclaim the good news of your justice, your jubilee year, the liberation of all from violence and death, and as I invite people to the way of the cross and undergo it myself, may others be consoled in the hope, joy, and confidence of your resurrection, in your coming reign of peace at hand here and now.

To be understood, as to understand—

May I not be focused on argument, anger, fury, resentment, self-righteousness, indignation, or arrogance, but rather, let me understand every one else, listen to their pain, feel their sorrow, know their burdens, share their hopes and joys, weep when they weep and rejoice when they rejoice, be attentive to their needs and always to put others first. Let me know every human being as my sister and brother.

To be loved, as to love—

Grant that I may not so much seek selfishly the love of others, insisting on my rights and needs, but instead, to love others selflessly, generously, beyond measure, unconditionally, without any desire for reciprocation, without any expectation of service in return: a love that is willing to suffer for others; that will lay down my life for others in the nonviolent struggle for peace, for justice for the poor, for protection of the earth and all living things; a love even for my enemies, my persecutors; a love that insists on truth, that resists evil nonviolently, that reflects your own love for all people, a love that radiates your love present in my own spirit calling me your beloved.

For it is in giving that we receive—

By giving selflessly, sacrificially, all that we have, as you did for us dying on the cross in the struggle for justice and truth; by sharing our resources with the poor, sharing our lives with one another, sharing our faith, hope, and love with all people we receive a hundred times more in life, love, friends, faith, hope, peace, and joy. We receive your blessing, your wisdom, your mercy, your love, your presence, You yourself.

It is in pardoning that we are pardoned—

That I may forgive everyone who has ever hurt me, especially those closest to me, my family, my friends, my community; that I may let go of all resentment, grudges, anger, bitterness, and hostility; that I may see only your love, present in everyone; concentrate on your abiding presence, and so love all; that I may grant clemency to all and so win clemency for myself and all; that I may pardon others as you have already pardoned me and continue to pardon me; that I may resist war, injustice, and poverty through the steadfast nonviolent resistance that risks my life yet already forgives all who persecute me, so that your reign of forgiveness and compassion may be proclaimed.

It is in dying that we are born to eternal life.

Through our own deaths, the peaceful letting go of our lives, every day of our lives, until our final breath, may we experience life and go deeper into new life; by entering your paschal mystery, by sharing in your cross—the way of nonviolent resistance to systemic injustice, the way of compassion and truth, justice and love, the way of redemptive love through unearned suffering, willingly accepted without even the desire for retaliation. By sharing in your death, Jesus, we are born into the new life of your resurrection and enter into the paradise of your peace to live with you, the saints, and the God of life, in perfect joy, forever and ever.

Amen. Alleluia.

I rest most of the morning in bed, not feeling well. I walk up for Sext prayers and dine on soup, fish, and vegetables. I return and read Gandhi. A quiet day. I speak with no one. A gray blanket covers the earth. The fire is roaring again, and I sit from 3–4 P.M., breathing in and out, confessing my sins to God, begging for mercy, asking for help, looking out the window, pondering the birchwood cross by the porch. I contemplate Jesus sitting before me, offering a final word of invitation, as he did to Peter: "Follow me." "If you let me, I will take you by the hand and lead you." I say yes and pray for the grace to follow him today, right now, for the rest of my life and forever.

I confess my inability to follow him on my own. I ask Jesus for the grace to go deeper into God, to get beyond my selfishness, ego, narcissism, sin, self-righteousness, arrogance, pride, and despair; to mature spiritually and humanly: to grow up. These things will happen gradually over time, I hear him say. I must stay close to him in prayer, in silence, in faith, closer than ever in the days and years ahead. I have no idea where I am going or what is happening to me or how I can be of service to others, but Christ will lead me and take me through my life and one day explain it to me when I finally reach his house of peace.

5:00 P.M. I walk northeast from the cottage, through the fields and the trees, up the hill and into the woods. From a greater height perhaps nearly a mile away, you can still see the hermitage. Hidden among the barren trees, I come upon an abandoned two room hermitage with a large dead tree fallen through its middle. The walls have caved in. The floors have rotted away. Who lived here alone in these woods? When did this house hear the prayers of the silent? How long has this hermitage stood in silent vigil?

Walking outside, I return to an old dream. Someday, I hope to join others in a peaceful satyagraha campaign aimed at the conversion of the Pentagon. This presence of prayer and protest would include weekly vigils and periodic civil disobedience. This vision keeps coming back to me. I spent much time reflecting on it while in jail for my Plowshares action. May it come true someday and help us usher in a new era of disarmament, nonviolence, and peace.

Again I sit. I read and walk. I fix the fire, clean the kitchen, and kneel before the altar offering intercessory prayers. It's 6:00. Night has fallen. I near the end of my stay. One week from now I will be back in the chaos of New York City.

How does one be a contemplative in a city of noise and activity? I don't know. I do know that I will need to get away periodically, certainly one weekend a month, to a quiet place, perhaps by the ocean or in the country. I also know the value of rising early in the morning and sitting in silent prayer. Finally, I must remember to pray throughout the day, to take time-out to dip again into that inner sacred space, as St. Ignatius advises in his examen, to breathe in and out mindfully, to return to my center, to enter Christ's peace. In this way, I can continue my journey in life, the interior journey to Christ and his reign of peace.

That is all I want for myself and for everyone. If there was a way I could make it happen, or proclaim it convincingly, or ensure it's coming, I would do it. Alas for such all-American aspirations! All I can do is fall on the ground and implore the mercy of Christ, to let it all happen—or not happen—in any case, to let it all be as Christ wishes.

As Merton told David Stendl-Rast a few days before flying off to Asia, "As a Christian, I intend to become a very good Buddhist."

Saturday

T oday is the first clear day in a week. Not a cloud in the sky. In this magnificent blue sky, the sun shines right over the hills and the fields and the trees into this hermitage. A white frost covers the ground. A hazy mist rests upon the hills. It is cold but not bitter, and in here, a blazing fire keeps the room toasty.

Within the hermitage, the silence, peace, and isolated beauty of my solitude hold me still. These hills and woods play host to the Spirit of Christ who keeps vigil here, too.

Last night, while I was reading the Psalms shortly after 6:00, a four wheel drive truck came roaring up the hill with its headlights cutting through the night. Out walks Fr. Carlos in Cistercian habit and blue jean denim coat, carrying a case of beer and a bag of aged Trappist cheese with crackers. We talked, laughed, and shared stories until 9 P.M. A celebration for both of us.

Carlos is from Manila and was a priest with the Society of the Divine Word for twenty-four years. He was popular in Manila and a leader in the order. At one point, he served as novice master for eighty-five newcomers. Then in the mid-1980s, he discerned a call to the life of silence, visited several monasteries, left his order, lived at the Abbey of the Genesee for two years, and finally found a home here at Gethsemani. He had been here only a year or two when we met in 1989, but now he is junior master, the superior of five scholastics (who have finished the novitiate but have several years of study before they profess final vows). He spent the day yesterday typing in orders for cheese and fruitcake. Yesterday alone, over eight hundred orders came through the mail. This three month period at the end of the year is the busiest time of all, and every monk works to keep the business going. Like Patrick, Carlos sits at the computer all day. He spends the time praying with love for each name that he enters into the computer.

We talk at length about prayer, monastic life, Christ, Merton, the good Abbot, Carlos' family, and the future. "I am so excited about the future," he shouts enthusiastically, his hands waving. "I can't wait to see what becomes of the church, but I know it will be new and different and good. And the world, too, and most of all, heaven! I can't wait. I have so much hope."

His energy was a shot of adrenalin. I need his enthusiasm, his hope, as I am perennially depressed about the future, the church, the world. I had to challenge him with my doubts. What about war, nuclear weapons, starvation, the inhumanity of it all, the corporate greed killing the poor of the world? He knows it all to well. When he lived in the Philippines, he actively resisted injustice, lead nonviolent demonstrations against Marcos in the 1960s, faced the gun barrels, visited the prisons, and every weekend for several decades served the most desperate poor in the slums of Manila.

"The main thing is Christ!" he exclaims. "We are all centered in Christ, and heading toward Christ and Christ's kingdom; and isn't that exciting!?" He looks at me with eyes wide open.

With that, we toast Christ. "Enjoy this feast," he urges me with a smile.

The stories he tells! A ninety-six-year-old monk who has been here all his life once told Carlos: "I'll never forget one incredible day when we all gathered for our weekly conference, and the Abbot looked at us and said slowly, 'World War II has begun. Let us begin our conference.'

"'What?' the monk asked himself. 'What World War II? What does that mean? What happened? What is happening out there?' Not a word was mentioned. We knew nothing. We were told nothing. Years and years went by, until one morning, as we were gathering for our regular community meeting, the Abbot walked in and announced, 'World War II has ended. Let us begin our conference. . . .'"

This morning at Mass, the Gospel cites Jesus' words about the resurrection to the Sadducees. "In the next age, [those who die] will be like angels," he says. "They will be sons and daughters of God, sons and daughters of resurrection." I pray that I may be instilled with resurrection, filled with the hope, joy, and life of the risen Lord; and that I may begin, from this day forward, to resist death in all its forms, to radiate the peace of the risen Christ and to live as a son of the resurrection, a son of God! What a glorious destiny.

I look up from my desk and witness a glorious panorama. This beautiful November morn sparkles with new life like Easter. The sunshine warms my hands. Again, I feel a deep peace.

> I lift up my eyes to the mountains; from where shall come my help? My help is from the Lord who made heaven and earth. (Ps 121:1–2)

> The farthest east and west you make resound with joy. You have visited the land and watered it; greatly have you enriched it. . . . The untilled meadows overflow with a rich harvest, and rejoicing clothes the hills. The fields are garmented with flocks and the valleys blanketed with grain. They shout and sing for joy. (Ps 65:9–14)

I have a good morning visit with Brother Patrick. Over coffee, he tells me about his latest publishing work about Thomas Merton and about his own family, his college years at Notre Dame, his four years as a member of the Holy Cross religious order before he came to Gethsemani in 1951.

"Why did you decide to leave Holy Cross and join the Trappists?" I ask.

"Because I read *The Seven Storey Mountain*," he answers. "That started it all for me."

We talk about the hermitage. "Merton had the place filled with book cases and four or five file cabinets. Books and papers lay everywhere, but he didn't keep any of his own books.

"I had been working at our Generalate in Rome in the mid-1960s," he continues, "and had an audience with Pope Paul VI. I presented him with a privately printed book by Merton on Cassiodorus. The Pope took it from my hands, kissed it, and clasped it to his chest, twisting his body left and right, and said with awe, 'Thomas Merton and Cassiodorus!' Then he presented an iron cross to me and said,

'Give this to Thomas Merton and tell him I got his letter and am thinking about the problem.' Merton had written with suggestions about certain Carmelite monasteries, and why they should know more about what was happening in the world."

When Patrick returned, Merton said to him, "Come up and see me in the hermitage." So Patrick walked up and presented Merton with the cross. Merton put it on the desk, walked out into the kitchen, returned with a frosted mug and a can of beer and offered them to Patrick. "This was typical Merton," Patrick concluded. "So kind and thoughtful and gracious."

Rightly so, I think, because you, too, Patrick, are kind and thoughtful and gracious. Your hospitality and generosity and warmth are all too rare.

I read Merton on Gandhi last night before falling asleep. The great key for Merton regarding Gandhi's nonviolence was that it sprang from a deep inner spiritual life, what Merton called Gandhi's "inner unity." "In Gandhi's mind, nonviolence was not simply a political tactic which was supremely useful and efficacious in liberating his people from foreign rule, in order that India might then concentrate on realizing its own national identity. On the contrary, the spirit of nonviolence sprang from an inner realization of spiritual unity in himself. The whole Gandhian concept of nonviolent action and satyagraha is incomprehensible if it is thought to be a means of achieving unity rather than as the fruit of inner unity already achieved."

Merton struggled hard to realize inner unity. I believe he reached it, and we are all still reaping the fruits of his true self, his inner unity, his satyagraha. I remember struggling with this question of inner unity during my visit seven years ago. What have I to show for the past seven years? Moments and whole seasons of great inner division. However, I have had glimpses of unity and have enjoyed some long periods of inner freedom in recent years that brought spiritual consolation. The burnout, despair, anxiety, and exhaustion that I experienced the past two years have been a kind of spiritual disaster for me. I lost my center.

This week, I have regained a peaceful spirit and spent glorious hours in this hermitage, at this desk, or sitting on the porch, on the edge of realization. Pure joy, perfect peace. I have been blessed by a grace given, unearned and undeserved, but given nonetheless, and I want to share it with others. I also want to learn from recent years and not make the same mistakes again in the future by allowing my insides to be torn to shreds.

I prayed for this grace last night in the middle of the night, and I ask for it again right now, that I may grow deeper in the spiritual life. Even though I am an active Jesuit priest, immersed in the problems of the world, the struggle against oppression, the protest against injustice, and the service of compassion to those in need, I pray to maintain a deep inner unity, to live out of my true self, to practice mindfulness, to breathe in and out the Spirit of Christ's peace, to be forever a son of the resurrection, a son of God.

Suddenly, the birds have appeared. It has turned into a spring morning. The air is filled with song.

A curious thing! While wrapped in a brown afghan and sitting in the rocking chair, enjoying the Buddhist present, savoring contemplative peace, I look out the window and see far in the distance on the horizon, a jet streak up from hills, flying far overhead, leaving a long white, vertical streak, a long white line dividing the blue sky directly in front of me. A few minutes later, another airplane, also some thirty-five thousand feet high, flies across the sky, this time from my left to right (East to West), leaving behind a long horizontal flume of white smoke.

Suddenly, in the blue sky hovers a large white cross, as if by the finger of God. The sky reminds me of the cross of my Lord, and my heart is full. Once again I hear the call to discipleship, to follow the crucified Christ, to take up the nonviolent cross in resistance to systemic injustice, to walk the way of redemptive suffering love, to risk public confrontation with the principalities and powers and undergo death without retaliation. Yes, I accept the cross. I proclaim it. Christ's cross is the only way to transform our unjust world and violent hearts into God's reign of justice and love.

Early afternoon. For some reason, when I went to check the wood-burning heater, a wave of black smoke came pouring out of the furnace, waking me from my reverie, forcing me out the front door and into the fresh air, where I discovered the temperature had climbed from around twenty degrees to sixty degrees or warmer in the sun. The bugs, bees, flies—even grasshoppers!—had thawed out and flew around everywhere. I sat behind the house on a ledge of large stones against the edge of the woods until some bees encircled me. Now I'm back on the porch, in the sun, content, coming back to life.

The monk's sense of time. Fr. Carlos recently read Carl Sagan in *Scientific American.* "Imagine," he says with childlike awe, "if the history of time were the length of a year and the big bang was in January, the neolithic age only occurred in December, and humans did not appear on the scene until

December 31, at 11:59 P.M. and fifty-three seconds. And you think your life is important? We are nothing in the grand scheme of things!"

Everything is charged with energy, from the sun to the breeze to the hills. I brought the rocking chair out onto the porch and sit in the sun, in the shadow of the cross. Looking through Merton's *Asian Journal*, rereading his experience at Polonnaruwa, I try to enter that same Buddhist enlightenment here in these woods. With eyes closed and a half-smile on my face, I breathe in peace. I breathe out peace. The sun warms my eyelids. Birds sing in the distance. The bells toll. A breeze blows the air on my face.

Time goes by. Then, I awake to discover I've been asleep. So much for keeping watch with Christ at Gethsemani! Like the other disciples, I sleep.

This leads me again to listen carefully to Christ's words, which I look up in the Gospel. "Watch and pray!" he tells Simon Peter (Mk 14:38). "Of that day or hour, no one knows, neither the angels in heaven, nor the Son, but only the Father. Be watchful! Be alert! You do not know when the time will come. It is like a man traveling abroad. He leaves home and places his servants in charge, each with his work, and orders the gatekeeper to be on the watch. Watch, therefore; you do not know when the lord of the house is coming, whether in the evening, or at midnight, or at cock-crow, or in the morning. May he not come suddenly and find you sleeping. What I say to you, I say to all: Watch!" (Mk 13:33–37).

The duty of the Christian in these atrocious times includes keeping watch as peacemaking contemplatives, as people of nonviolence in a culture of violence, with our hearts and minds ever ready to welcome the God of peace. We prepare for the nonviolent coming of our unarmed God by disarming ourselves. We look for God's presence in our midst. We attend God's Holy Spirit of peace among us by pursuing peace between us at every moment.

In this Kentucky solitude, the monks watch and pray. They mark the hours with laudes at cockcrow, vigils and Mass in the morning, sext and none during the day, vespers and compline in the evening and night. What is our contemplative equivalent, we Christians who take our chances in the world? How do we keep watch? How do we pray? What are we watching for? Do we wait and watch for the Christ, the living God? Or have we given into the culture's myth of progress? Do we look for better days ahead, trusting in the false wisdom of Wall Street, Hollywood, and the Pentagon?

Here in the woods, there are no more questions. The grasshoppers, the birds, the trees are in the land beyond questions. They live in the present. They see all and do not react. They are themselves and, thus, reach the fullness of their being. They are true contemplatives. They keep watch for us, since we as a people have abandoned our vocation.

What is the sound of listening? It is the rustle of leaves among the top branches in the woods of Mt. Olivet. It is the sweet song of the bird at sunset singing its praise. It is wind blowing through the pine trees. It is the gentle play of fallen leaves, leap-frogging over one another along the grass. It is the toll of the monastery bells at Gethsemani, saying, "Not my will, but your will be done. Watch and pray that you may not be put to the test." It is a whisper from the solitude of God: "Here is my servant whom I uphold, my chosen one with whom I am pleased, upon whom I have put my spirit, the one who shall bring forth justice to the nations" (Is 42:1). "Come my beloved, and share my life in the house of peace."

❖

You have favored, O God, your land;
You have restored the well-being of Jacob.
You have forgiven the guilt of your people;
You have covered all their sins.
You have withdrawn all your wrath;
You have revoked your burning anger.
Restore us, O God, our savior, and abandon your displeasure
    with us. . . .
Will you not give us life; and shall not your people rejoice in
    you?
Show us, O God, your kindness, and grant us your salvation.
I will hear what God proclaims,
for God proclaims peace
to God's people, to God's faithful ones, to those who put in
    God their hope.
Near indeed is God's salvation to those who fear God,
Glory dwelling in our land.
Kindness and Truth shall meet;
Justice and Peace shall kiss.
Truth shall spring out of the earth,
Justice shall look down from heaven.
God will give God's benefits;
our land shall yield its increase.
Justice shall walk before God
and salvation, along the way of God's steps. (Ps 85)

When the practice of nonviolence becomes universal,
God will reign on earth as God does in heaven.

—Gandhi

3:00 P.M. A white pick-up truck pulls up in front of the hermitage. Two young men and an elderly monk start unloading a pile of chopped wood. I introduce myself. Brother Ambrose is seventy-one years old and came to Gethsemani in 1942, two months after Merton. He is short with a long white beard and a bald head, and he looks like an Indian Hindu yogi.

He immediately asks about myself and tells me about the hermitage and Merton. He was the first monk in the community to make a retreat here after Merton's death, a practice that continues. Each week, a different monk makes a one week silent retreat in solitude here. He spoke of the changes he's seen over the years, but, he said with a smile, we came here for God and we stay for God and God has never changed.

After we unloaded the wood and said goodbye, a giant green tractor pulling a huge round metal water container appeared over the hill and parked right next to the hermitage. Out comes Brother Conrad, and we talk for thirty minutes. He's from a family of twelve, was born and raised in Kentucky, entered the monastery in 1957, and speaks with a thick Southern accent.

He speaks fondly of Merton. "I used to attend Father Louis's [Merton's] talks to the community," he says. "In those days, I was the cellarer and passed on extra food and beer for Merton to take back up to the hermitage. The thing about Merton was, he was a very humble man." After a long pause, he grins and adds, "unlike most well-educated folk."

For decades, Brother Conrad worked on the farm. Then, "on July 25, 1992," he says solemnly, "Father Abbot called me into the office and told me I would be running the cheese factory from now on. I had never worked there and didn't know anything about it."

It began to get chilly, and I commented on the weather. "In the old days, when Merton was here, this place had no plumbing or electricity," Brother said.

"That must have been hard to endure," I replied.

He gave me along steady look. "No, Father, you get used to it. My whole family grew up without heat, electricity, running water, or plumbing. I never had any of that until I came here."

A good, decent, wise, simple man—the best of Kentucky. A person without guile. I am grateful to have met these two holy monks.

I spent the whole day sitting on the porch, walking in the woods around the house, and writing at this desk, a day spent keeping vigil. What comes of such a day? It heals, unifies, soothes, and energizes. It offers a peace that melts away fears, insecurities and violence, and fills me with faith, hope, and love. It is a gift. Today, I spent the day with Christ in Gethsemani.

This afternoon, I sat from 4–5:30 in the rocker on the porch looking at the hills, read the scriptures, cleaned up, built a fire, and then sat in prayer for an hour. Now at 8 P.M., at Merton's desk, I am tired. Alone here in the woods, I do not look forward to going back into the world. I tell God that I fear returning to my old, worst self—arrogant, proud, resentful, fearful, insecure, selfish, unloving, despairing, and faithless. But Jesus is consoling. "I have brought you here," he says, "and I have other places I will bring you. And I will be with you the whole way. I love you. Do not be afraid. Trust me. Cheer up."

Well, then, I am ready. For this week, these holy days, this house, the hospitality of the Trappist community, and the generosity of my own community, most of all for my encounter with the God of peace on this mountaintop, I give thanks.

I hear the monks finishing Compline. Let us bless the Lord, the cantor sings.

"Thanks be to God," I sing in the silence of the hermitage.

The house knows the hymn. It is practiced in the art of listening.

Sunday, November 24, 1996:
The Feast of Christ the King

I wake up at 4 A.M. and lie in bed until 7:30. Despair and discouragement creep up on me, sadness at my imminent departure, a sudden remembrance of the burdens and sorrows which await, as well as the unknown future. I think of Merton who lay awake under this icon of the Nativity in this corner room in the silence of these woods. I touch the icon and receive its blessing.

The place is clean, and I'm ready to go. I sit in the chair by the fire looking out the window for one last hour. The peace remains as intense, as still as ever. I pray that I may retain the inner freedom of Merton's hermitage, that I may live always in the inner house of peace, and pursue the sound of listening. I look to Christ and listen for his voice. He is here. I take heart and head out the door, after giving thanks in the chapel.

I make my way across the field and turn back once, in amazement and gratitude. The land of silence, the land of peace! I descend the mountain a new man, for I have tasted the peace of resurrection. I have heard the still, small voice of God. I have looked to the hills from whence comes my help. I have met my true self, encountered the risen Lord and rejoiced. I go now to tell my sisters and brothers that he goes ahead of us, that he sends his peace, that we shall see him.

Brother Patrick meets me with coffee and asks about my day and my plans. I thank him for these glorious days and for the great gift he has given the church by keeping alive the memory and writings of Thomas Merton. The resurgence and interest are due in large part to Patrick's steadfast, faithful, scholarly support of Merton's legacy. Merton and his message will live on, I think, because of this faithful servant. We say good bye. He gives me the peace sign. Thank you, dear friend.

Mass for the feast of Christ the King begins with a beautiful hymn: "Light here scatters all our darkness! Life here triumphs over death! Come, receive from Christ in glory God the Spirit's living breath! Praise Christ for his victory won!"

The Abbot calls us to prayer. "May we who are poor always serve Christ in the poor and needy and one day enter his kingdom." He blesses us with holy water as the crowded congregation sings, "The waters of the river give joy to God's city. God is within, it cannot be shaken." We hear God speak to us as a shepherd, saying, "I myself will look after and tend my sheep. As a shepherd tends his flock when he finds himself among his scattered sheep, so will I tend my sheep. I will rescue them from every place where they are scattered when it was cloudy and dark. I myself will pasture my sheep; I myself will give them rest. The lost I will seek out, the strayed I will bring back, the injured I will bind up, the sick I will heal, shepherding them rightly" (Ez 34:11–12, 15–17).

In response, we sing from Psalm 121, "I rejoiced when I heard them say, 'Let us go to God's house.'" Then, the second reading from Paul's first letter to the Corinthians proclaims, "Christ is raised from the dead. . . . In Christ, all will come to life again" (I Cor 15:20–26).

The grand gospel parable of the Last Judgment is read slowly and carefully. "The king will say to those on his right: 'Come. You have my Father's blessing! Inherit the kingdom prepared for you from the creation of the world. For I was hungry and you gave me food, I was thirsty and you gave me drink. I was a stranger and you welcomed me, naked and you clothed me. I was ill and you comforted me, in prison and you came to visit me . . . I assure you, as often as you did this to one of my least brothers and sisters, you did it to me" (Mt 25:31–46).

These words have become a living ikon, a talisman for Christian life. What we do to one another, especially to the poor, we do to Christ. The opposite brings the lesson home: What we do not do for the poor, we do not do for Christ. I ponder the world we live in to shed light on the Word. The culture around us promotes the anti-kingdom. For example, it makes people hungry and thirsty, poor and naked. In our country, we cut funding for the poor and spend our resources for new prisons. We do not spend the necessary resources to cure AIDS or develop adequate health care for all. Instead, we pollute our water, destroy the environment, and turn away the stranger. Such inhumanity reaches its climax in war, as Dorothy Day and Daniel Berrigan explain. The whole purpose of war is to kill the enemy, and if the enemy can not be killed, at least, war makes the enemy poor, hungry, thirsty, naked, homeless, sick, and puts them in prison. But in our times, we are intent on destroying the entire earth with our nuclear weapons, our toxic waste, our destruction of the environment. We will wipe out the entire pasture, sheep, goats, shepherd—the works. The culture will not be satisfied until Christ in the poor and in the enemy is dead and gone.

The Word of God calls us to see Christ then, not only in the poor, but in our enemies. If we want to know where God is in our broken world, we need not look farther than the suffering people around us. There stands Christ. I pray that the Lord will forgive us, have mercy on us, and help us come to our senses. I hope we will serve Christ present in the poor, hungry, homeless, displaced, sick, imprisoned, and marginalized. More, that we will abolish war forever, dismantle every weapon of destruction, melt down every gun, demolish every prison, and teach one another nonviolent ways of being human.

As I receive communion and praise God, I look around the altar at these good monks and at the faithful congregation who come to worship the God of silence. My spirit is lifted as together we bless our God. Like incense rising to heaven, our prayers rise.

I walk out of the sanctuary renewed. The sun is shining. The prayer continues.

Apostles' Creed: Updated

I believe in God, Creator of heaven and earth,
    the God of peace,
    the God of justice,
    the God of compassion,
    the God of nonviolence,
    the God who is our Father and our Mother,
    Mercy within Mercy within Mercy,
    Love beyond measure.

I believe in Jesus Christ, our savior and redeemer, brother and
    friend.
    In the Spirit of peace, Jesus was born of Mary—
    mother of the poor, mother of the homeless, mother of
    peace.
    He gathered friends together, healed the broken-hearted,
    liberated the oppressed, and preached good news to the
    poor.
    He called us all to love one another, to love our enemies,

to speak truth, to make peace, to seek justice,
to put away the sword of violence and take up the cross
of nonviolence,
to prefer voluntary suffering to inflicting pain or killing
others;
peace to war; life to death.
He turned over the tables of systemic injustice.
He resisted the culture of violence and walked the way
of nonviolence.
The principalities and powers had him arrested, jailed,
tried, tortured, and executed.
A victim of the death penalty, he suffered, died, and was
buried.
On the third day, he rose again.
"Peace be with you," he says as he shows us his wounds.
He ascended into heaven and sits at the right hand of
the God of nonviolence.
With love, truth, and compassion, he judges the living
and the dead.
He wipes away every tear, every fear, and every trace of
death.
He hosts a wedding feast, an eternal celebration of life
for all.
His realm of nonviolence, peace, and justice will have no
end.

I believe in the Holy Spirit,
the Spirit of peace and nonviolence,
the Spirit of truth and love,
the Spirit of life,
the Spirit of resistance and reconciliation,
the Spirit of forgiveness and compassion,
the Spirit who leads us to beat swords into plowshares,

to seek justice, make peace, and dwell at one with all
   creation.

I believe in God, Creator, Redeemer, and Sanctifier,
   the God who calls us together in a holy Catholic
      Church—
   welcoming all, including all, embracing all—
   a community of faith, hope, and love,
   a community of nonviolence,
   a community of resisters and peacemakers,
   a community of children, women, and men,
   black, brown, red, yellow, and white,
   of every variety and age and land—
   to walk together in peace and love.

I believe that we shall join the communion of saints,
   from Mary and Joseph, Peter and Paul,
   to Francis and Claire,
   Ignatius Loyola and Therese of Lisieux,
   to Dorothy Day and Mohandas Gandhi,
   Martin Luther King, Jr. and Thea Bowman,
   Oscar Romero and Ignacio Ellacuria,
   Franz Jaegerstaetter and Thomas Merton,
   Ita Ford and Maura Clarke,
   Dorothy Kazel and Jean Donovan,
   and the whole cloud of witnesses—
   all martyrs, prophets, apostles, and peacemakers—
   the whole of humanity in the great dance of life.
   I believe we are forgiven and called to forgive one another.

I believe in the God of life and resurrection.

I believe, God.

Help my unbelief.

Amen. Alleluia.

About the Author

John Dear is a Jesuit priest, peace activist, and executive director of the Fellowship of Reconciliation, the largest, oldest interfaith peace organization in the United States. He has worked among the poor and needy in Washington, D.C., Richmond, Virginia, and El Salvador; taught theology at Fordham University; and spent eight months in prison from 1993–94 for a Plowshares anti-nuclear demonstration. From 1997–98, he lived in Derry, Northern Ireland, and worked at a human rights center in Belfast. His other books include *Peace Behind Bars; Disarming the Heart; The God of Peace; The Sacrament of Civil Disobedience;* and *Seeds of Nonviolence.* He has edited works by or about Daniel Berrigan, Henri Nouwen, and Mairead Corrigan Maguire. He currently lives in New York City.

To join the Fellowship of Reconciliation or to receive its magazine, *Fellowship,* contact:

FOR, Box 271, Nyack, NY 10960
Telephone: (914) 358-4601
Website: www. nonviolence.org